# PYTHON INSTITUTE
Open Education & Development Group

# CERTIFICATE

of proficiency in the
Python programming language

**Robert Method Karamagi**

PCEP - Certified Entry-Level Python Programmer

Verify this certificate's authenticity at
verify.openedg.org

Certification Code: **ARoQ.64HC.qh8x**

Exam Version: **PCEP-30-01 [NP]**

Date Certified: **December 30, 2021**

Scope:

- Basic Programming Concepts, Techniques and Best Practices
- Data Types, Evaluations, and Basic Input-Output Operations
- Flow Control: Loops, and Conditional Blocks
- Data Collections: Lists, Tuples, and Dictionaries
- Functions

Christopher Boguslawski
President, Python Institute

2

# PCEP – Certified Entry-Level Python Programmer Certification Overview

**PCEP – Certified Entry-Level Python Programmer** certification is a professional credential that measures your ability to accomplish coding tasks related to the essentials of programming in the Python language. A test candidate should demonstrate sufficient knowledge of the universal concepts of computer programming, the syntax and semantics of the Python language as well as the skills in resolving typical implementation challenges with the help of the Python Standard Library.

**PCEP – Certified Entry-Level Python Programmer** certification shows that the individual is familiar with universal computer programming concepts like data types, containers, functions, conditions, loops, as well as Python programming language syntax, semantics, and the runtime environment.

Becoming PCEP certified ensures that the individual is acquainted with the most essential means provided by Python 3 to enable her/him to start their own studies at an intermediate level and to continue their professional development.

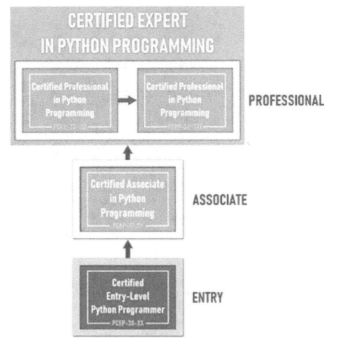

**PCEP – Certified Entry-Level Python Programmer** certification is an interim step to the PCAP – Certified Associate in Python Programming certification and the starting point to launch a career in software development, Python programming, and related technologies. Becoming PCEP certified will help you stand out from other candidates and get your foot in the door.

**PCEP: Exam Information**

- Exam name: PCEP Certified Entry-Level Python Programmer
- Exam Code/Exam Version: PCEP-30-01 | Status: Published
- Exam Level: Entry
- Associated Certifications: PCAP – Certified Associate in Python programming (PCAP-31-02, PCAP-31-01)
- Pre-requisites: None
- Duration: 45 minutes (exam) + approx. 5 minutes (Non-Disclosure Agreement/Tutorial)
- Number of Questions: 30

- Format: Single-choice and multiple-choice questions, drag & drop, gap fill | Python 3.x
- Passing Score: 70%
- Language: English
- Courses Aligned: PCAP: Programming Essentials in Python (Cisco Networking Academy, instructor-led: Modules 1-3), PCAP: Programming Fundamentals in Python (Part 1) – OpenEDG Education Platform, self-enroll/self-study
- Full Exam Price: USD 59
- Delivery Channel: OpenEDG Testing Service
- Testing Policies: Click here to view Testing Policies
- Exam Syllabus: Click here to view Exam Syllabus
- Sample Test: Click here to download a free PCEP sample test (TBA)

## Exam Objectives

The test candidate should demonstrate the sufficient knowledge of the following concepts:

**1.** The fundamentals of computer programming, i.e. how the computer works, how the program is executed, how the programming language is defined and constructed, what the difference is between compilation and interpretation, what Python is, how it is positioned among other programming languages, and what distinguishes the different versions of Python;

**2.** The basic methods of formatting and outputting data offered by Python, together with the primary kinds of data and numerical operators, their mutual relations and bindings; the concept of variables and variable naming conventions; the assignment operator, the rules governing the building of expressions; the inputting and converting of data;

**3.** Boolean values to compare difference values and control the execution paths using the *if* and *if-else* instructions; the utilization of loops (*while* and *for*) and how to control their behavior using the *break* and *continue* instructions; the difference between logical and bitwise operations; the concept of lists and list processing, including the iteration provided by the *for* loop, and slicing; the idea of multi-dimensional arrays;

**4.** The defining and using of functions – their rationale, purpose, conventions, and traps; the concept of passing arguments in different

ways and setting their default values, along with the mechanisms of returning the function's results; name scope issues; new data aggregates: tuples and dictionaries, and their role in data processing.

**Exam block #1: Basic Concepts (17%)**
**Objectives covered by the block** (5 exam items)
- fundamental concepts: interpreting and the interpreter, compilation and the compiler, language elements, lexis, syntax and semantics, Python keywords, instructions, indenting
- literals: Boolean, integer, floating-point numbers, scientific notation, strings
- comments
- the print() function
- the input() function
- numeral systems (binary, octal, decimal, hexadecimal)
- numeric operators: ** * / % // + −
- string operators: * +
- assignments and shortcut operators

**Exam block #2: Data Types, Evaluations, and Basic I/O Operations (20%)**
**Objectives covered by the block** (6 exam items)
operators: unary and binary, priorities and binding
bitwise operators: ~ & ^ | << >>
Boolean operators: **not and or**
Boolean expressions
relational operators ( == != > >= < <= ), building complex Boolean expressions
accuracy of floating-point numbers
basic input and output operations using the **input(), print(), int(), float(), str(), len()** functions
formatting **print()** output with **end=** and **sep=** arguments
type casting
basic calculations
simple strings: constructing, assigning, indexing, immutability

**Exam block #3: Flow Control – loops and conditional blocks (20%)**
**Objectives covered by the block** (6 exam items)
- conditional statements: **if, if-else, if-elif, if-elif-else**
- multiple conditional statements

- the **pass** instruction
- building loops: **while, for, range()**, **in**
- iterating through sequences
- expanding loops: **while-else, for-else**
- nesting loops and conditional statements
- controlling loop execution: **break, continue**

**Exam block #4: Data Collections – Lists, Tuples, and Dictionaries (23%)**
**Objectives covered by the block** (7 exam items)

- simple lists: constructing vectors, indexing and slicing, the **len()** function
- lists in detail: indexing, slicing, basic methods (**append(), insert(), index()**) and functions (**len(), sorted()**, etc.), **del** instruction, iterating lists with the **for** loop, initializing, **in** and **not** **in** operators, list comprehension, copying and cloning
- lists in lists: matrices and cubes
- tuples: indexing, slicing, building, immutability
- tuples vs. lists: similarities and differences, lists inside tuples and tuples inside lists
- dictionaries: building, indexing, adding and removing keys, iterating through dictionaries as well as their keys and values, checking key existence, **keys(), items()** and **values()** methods
- strings in detail: escaping using the \ character, quotes and apostrophes inside strings, multiline strings, basic string functions.

**Exam block #5: Functions (20%)**
**Objectives covered by the block** (6 exam items)

- defining and invoking your own functions and generators
- **return** and **yield** keywords, returning results,
- the **None** keyword,
- recursion
- parameters vs. arguments,
- positional keyword and mixed argument passing,
- default parameter values
- converting generator objects into lists using the **list()** function
- name scopes, name hiding (shadowing), the **global** keyword

# Contents

# Practice Exam 1

1. What will the output be after executing the following code snippet?
```
print(9** 3 ** 0 ** 1)
```
A. 3
B. 9
C. 1
D. 18

2. What will the output be, if we run the following code?
```
weekdays = ("Monday","Tuesday","Wednesday","Thursday")
weekdays.append("Friday")
print (weekdays)
```
A. Monday, Tuesday, Wednesday, Thursday
B. Friday
C. None
D. AttributeError: 'tuple' object has no attribute 'append'

3. How many times will it print "#"?
```
if x!=10:
   print("#")
   if x<8:
     print("#")
   elif x==10:
     print("#")
   else:
     print("#")
else:
   print("#"*3)
```
A. 3
B. 1
C. 2
D. 4

4. What is the output of this code when "robert" is entered by the user when prompted?
```
name = input()
print(name == " Robert ")
```
A. True

B. error

C. Robert

D. False

5. What would be printed to the console after the following code is executed?

```
i=0
while i < 1:
    print('Hello', end=", ")
    i += 1
else:
    print("World")
```

A. Hello

B. "Hello", World

C. Hello World

D. Hello, World

6. What will the output be after executing the following code?

```
Tupl = ['Python', 'Tuple']
print(tuple(Tupl))
```

A. ('Python', 'Tuple')

B. [Python, Tuple]

C. ['Python', 'Tuple']

D. (Python, Tuple)

7. What is the output when the following code snippet is run:

```
milk_left = "None"
if milk_left:
    print("Groceries trip pending!")
else:
    print("Let's enjoy a bowl of cereals")
```

A. Error

B. None

C. Let's enjoy a bowl of cereals

D. Groceries trip pending

8. What will the output be after executing the following code?

```
def put(x):
    return [6]

val = [0, 1, 2, 3, 4, 5]
```

```
y = put(val);
print(y)
```
A. [6]
B. [0, 1, 2, 3, 4, 5]
C. -6
D. (0,1,2,3,4)

9. What will the output be after executing the following code?
```
Dict = dict({1: 'Python', 2: 'Dictionaries'})
print(Dict)
```
A. dict{'Python', 'Dictionaries'}
B. dict({'Python', 'Dictionaries'})
C. {'Python', 'Dictionaries'}
D. {1: 'Python', 2: 'Dictionaries'}

10. What is the output of this code after the user inputs "Python" when prompted?
```
word = input()
print(word*3)
```
A. PythonPythonPython
B. error
C. Python*3
D. Python Python Python

11. What will the output be after running the following code?
```
def put(x):
  x[-1] = 6
val = [0, 1, 2, 3, 4, 5]
put(val);
print(val)
```
A. [0,1,2,3,4,5]
B. (0,1,2,3,4,5,6)
C. [0, 1, 2, 3, 4, 6]
D. [1,2,3,4,5,6]

12. What will the output be, if we execute the following code?
```
Dict = {'Name': 'Python', 1: [1, 2, 3, 4], 2: "hi"}
print(Dict)
```
A. {'Name': 'Python', [1, 2, 3, 4], 'hi'}
B. {'Name': 'Python', 1: [1, 2, 3, 4], 2: 'hi'}
C. Syntax Error

D.  {'Python', [1, 2, 3, 4], 'hi'}

13. What will the output be, if we run the following code?
```
lst1 = [0,1]
lst2 = [1,0]
for x in lst1:
    for y in lst2:
        print(x,y)
```

A.
```
0 1
1 1
0 0
1 0
```

B.
```
0 1
0 0
1 1
1 0
```

C.
```
0 1
0 0
1 0
1 1
```

D.
```
0 1
1 1
1 0
0 0
```

14. What will the output be after executing the following code?
```
print("Hello","\nPython!")
```
A.  Hello "\nPython!"
B.  Hello Python!
C.  Hello
    Python!
D.  Hello \nPython!

15. What will the output be after running the following code snippet?
full_name = "robert method karamagi"
print(full_name.title())
A.  Robert method karamagi
B.  Robert method Karamagi
C.  Robert Method Karamagi
D.  ROBERT METHOD KARAMAGI

16. What will the output be after calling the following function?
def sum(a,b):
 return a * b
 return a + b
print(sum(2,3))
A.  6
B.  Syntax Error
C.  6 5
D.  5

17. What will the output be after running the following code snippet?
age = 19
print(not age > 18 and age < 20)
A.  19
B.  SyntaxError
C.  True
D.  False

18. What would be printed to the console after the following code is executed?
for num in range(1, 10, 2):
   print(num, end = ",")
A.  2,4,6,8,10
B.  2,4,6,8
C.  1,3,5,7,9
D.  1,3,7,9

19. What will the output be after executing the following code snippet?
programming_language = "Python 3"
print (programming_language[-1])
A.  Nothing is printed
B.  3
C.  -1

D. P

20. What will the output be, if we run the following code?
dict1 = {1:"One", 2:"Two"}
dict1[2] = "One"
print(dict1)
A. No Output
B. {1: One, 2: Two}
C. {1:"One", 2:"One"}
D. {1: "One",1 : "One"}

21. What will the output be after running the following code?
nums = [1, 2, 3, 4, 5, 6, 7]
print(nums[::-1])
A. [1, 2, 3, 4, 5, 6]
B. [7, 6, 5, 4, 3, 2, 1]
C. [0, 1, 2, 3, 4, 5, 6]
D. [7, 1, 2, 3, 4, 5, 6]

22. What is the output of this code when 'wi' and 'fi' are entered by the user when prompted and stored in a and b, respectively?
a = input()
b = input()
print(a + b * 3)
A. wifiwiwifi
B. wifiwifiwifi
C. wifififi
D. wififififi

23. What will the output be after executing the following code?
print("Hello","World","Python", sep="#")
A. Hello#World#Python
B. error
C. #Hello#World#Python
D. HelloWorldPython#

24. What is the output of the following code?
print (5//4)
A. error
B. 4
C. 2

D. 1

25. What is the output of the following code?
num = 4,
print(type(num))
A. error
B. <class 'int'>
C. <class 'tuple'>
D. Invalid Data Type

26. What will the output be after running the following code?
```
def oddoreven(num):
  if (num % 2 == 0):
    print('even')
  else:
    print("odd")

oddoreven(13)
```
A. odd
B. even

27. What will the output be after running the following code?
```
def swap(x, y):
    z = x;
    x = y;
    y = z;
x = 5
y = 10
swap(x, y)
print(x , y)
```
A. error
B. 5 10
C. 10 5
D. Prints nothing

28. What will the output be after running the following code?
```
def default(x, y=5):
    print( y , x)
default(1)
```

A. Prints nothing

B. 1 5
C. error
D. 5 1

29. Will the following code run without errors?
tup1 = (1,3,5)
tup2 = (2,4)

tup1 = tup1+tup2
print(tup1)

A. This code will run without errors.
B. This code will not run.

30. What is the output after executing the following code?
fruits = ["Apples", "Oranges", "Mangoes"]
for fruit in fruits:
    if fruit != "Apples":
        print(fruit, end=" ")
A. Oranges Mangoes
B. Apple Mangoes
C. Apple Oranges
D. Apple Oranges Mangoes

# Practice Exam 2

1. What do you expect the following code will print given the first input is apple (stored in variable a) and the second input is banana (stored in variable b)?

```
a = input()
b = input()

x, y = b, a
print(x, y,sep="::")
```
A. apple:banana
B. apple::banana
C. banana:apple:
D. banana::apple

2. What will the output be after running the following code snippet?

```
def myfun(num):
    if num >= 4:
        return num
    else:
        return myfun(1) * myfun(2)

print(myfun(4))
```
A. 0
B. 4
C. 2
D. 1

3. What will the output be after running the following code snippet?

```
lst = ["apples","bananas", ""]
lst.remove("apples")
print(lst)
```
A. ['bananas', '']
B. ['bananas']
C. ['apples']
D. ['apples', 'bananas', '']

4. What will the output be after running the following code snippet?

```
nums = [1, 2, 3, 4, 5, 6, 7]
```

```
print(nums[::-1])
```
A. [7, 6, 5, 4, 3, 2, 1]
B. [1, 2, 3, 4, 5, 6, 7]
C. [1, 2, 3, 4, 5, 6]
D. [2, 3, 4, 5, 6, 7]

5. What will the output be after running the following code snippet?
```
a = 0b1011
b = 0b1001
print(bin(a ^ b))
```
A. 0b01
B. 0b11
C. 0b10
D. 10

6. What is the output of the following program?
```
x = 0
for i in range(10):
  for j in range(-1, -10, -1):
    x += 1
print(x)
```
A. 1
B. 9
C. 10
D. 90

7. What will the output be after running the following code snippet?
```
lst1 = [1, 4, 8, 16]
lst2 = [4, 16, 8, 1]

print(lst1 == lst2)
```
A. Not equal
B. Equal
C. False
D. True

8. What will the output be after running the following code snippet?
```
print(9 % 2 ** 4)
```
A. 4
B. error
C. 1

D. 9

9. What is the output of the following snippet of code:
```
def func(num):
  while num > 0:
    num = num - 1
num=3
func(num)
```
A.  2
B.  3
C.  Nothing is printed
D.  0

10. What will the output be after running the following code snippet?
```
if 1 == 1.0:
  print("Values are the same")
else:
  print("Values are different")
```
A.  Values are the same
B.  Values are different
C.  true
D.  false

11. What do you expect the following code to print:
```
nums = [1, 2, 3, 4]
nums.append(5)
print(nums)
```
A.  [5, 4, 3, 2, 1]
B.  [1, 2, 3, 4, 5]
C.  [1, 2, 3, 4]
D.  [5, 1, 2, 3, 4]

12. What will the output be after running the following code snippet?
```
x = 100
def glob():
  global x
  x = 20
glob()
print(x)
```
A.  100
B.  20

C. error
D. x not defined

13. What will the output be after running the following code snippet?
```
nums = [1, 2, 3]
for i in range(len(nums)):
    nums.insert(i,i+1)
print(nums)
```
A. [1, 1, 2, 2, 3, 3]
B. [1, 2, 3, 1, 2, 3]
C. [1, 2, 3, 3, 2, 1]
D. [1, 2, 3]

14. What will the output be after executing the following code snippet?
```
i = 0
while i > 3:
    i+=1
    print("Yes")
else:
    i -=1
    print("No")
```
A. error
B. Yes
C. No
D. 0

15. What will the output be after running the following code snippet?
```
s1="Hello Prof Karamagi"
print(s1.capitalize())
```
A. hello prof karamagi
B. HelloProfKaramagi
C. Hello prof karamagi
D. Hello Prof Karamagi

16. What will the output be after running the following code snippet?
```
t1 = (1, 2, 3)
t2 = ('apples', 'banana', 'pears')
print(t1 + t2)
```
A. (1, 2, 3), ('apples', 'banana', pears')
B. (1, 2, 3) + ('apple', 'banana'. 'pears')
C. (1, 2, 3, 'apples', 'banana', 'pears')

D. ('apple, 'banana', 'pears', 1, 2, 3)

17. What will happen if the following snippet of code is executed?

```python
def greeting(name= ""):
    print("Hello", name)

greeting()
```

A. Hello ""
B. Hello "name"
C. Hello, name
D. Hello

18. What will the output be after running the following code snippet?

```python
print("Robert","Karamagi", sep=",")
```

A. Robert,Karamagi
B. Robert ","Karamagi
C. Robert Karamagi
D. RobertKaramagi

19. What will the output be after running the following code snippet?

```python
marks = 55
if marks > 70 and marks < 80:
    print("First Class")
elif marks > 60 and marks < 70:
    print("Second Class")
elif marks >50 and marks < 60:
    print("Third Class")
else:
    print("No Class")
```

A. No Class
B. First Class
C. Second Class
D. Third Class

20. What will the output be after running the following code snippet?

```python
def tripler(num):
    def doubler(num):
        return num *2
    num = doubler(num)
    return num * 3
```

```
print(tripler(2))
```
A. 64
B. 12
C. 7
D. 6

21. What will the output be after running the following code snippet?
```
print(end='',sep='--')
```
A. --
B. ''
C. Nothing; no newline/blankline
D. '--'

22. What will the output be after running the following code snippet?
```
nums = [[1, 2, 3]]
initializer = 1

for i in range(1):
    initializer *= 10
    for j in range(1):
        nums[i][j] *= initializer

print(nums)
```
A. [[10, 2, 3]]
B. [[1, 2, 3]]
C. [[10, 1, 2, 3]]
D. [[10]]

23. What will the output be after running the following code snippet?
```
val = 5
print("less than 10") if val < 10 else print("greater than 10")
```
A. not valid
B. greater than 10
C. less than 10
D. syntax error

24. What will the output be after running the following code snippet?
```
d = {'one':2,'two':2}
d['one'] = 1
print(d)
```

A. {'one': 0, 'two': 1}
B. {'one': 0, 'two': 2}
C. {'one': 1, 'two': 2}
D. {'one': 1, 'two': 0}

25. What will the output be after running the following code snippet?
```
print("Python"*2,sep=',')
```
A. Python,Python
B. Python','Python
C. PythonPython
D. Python,*2

26. What will the output be after running the following code snippet?
```
def myprint(*val):
  print(val)
myprint("Peter","Piper","Pickled","Pepper")
```
A. error
B. ('Peter', 'Piper', 'Pickled', 'Pepper')
C. ('Peter')
D. ['Peter', 'Piper', 'Pickled', 'Pepper']

27. What do you expect to be output to the console?
```
if not(True):
 print("Hello, World!")
else:
 print("Python is Awesome!")
```
A. false
B. true
C. Python is Awesome!
D. Hello, World!

28. What will the output be after running the following code snippet?
```
print (10/5)
```
A. error
B. 2
C. 2.0
D. 5

29. What do you expect the following code snippet to printout:
```
tupl = tuple('Python World!')
print(tupl[:-7])
```

A. ('P', 'y', 't', 'h', 'o', 'n')
B. ('W', 'o', 'r', 'l', 'd', '!')
C. ('n', 'o', 'h', 't', 'y', 'P')
D. [P, y, t, h, o, n]

30. What will the output be after running the following code snippet?

```
def fun(a = 3, b = 2):
    return b ** a

print(fun(2))
```

A. 6
B. 4
C. 9
D. error

# Practice Exam 3

1. What will be the output after running the following code?

```
def func1():
    print("func1")
    def func2():
        print("func3")
        def func3():
            print("func3")
        func3()
    func2()
func1()
```

A.
```
func1
func3
func3
```

B.
```
func3
func3
func1
```

C.
```
func1
func2
func3
```

D.
```
func3
func2
func1
```

2. What will be the output after running the following code?
```
nums = [1, 2, 3, 4, 5, 6, 7]
print(nums[::-5])
```
A.  [7, 2]
B.  [7, 6, 5, 4, 3, 2]
C.  [7, 3]

D. SyntaxError

3. What will be the output after running the following code?
```
for i in range(10,12,2):
  if i % 2 != 1:
   print("No")
  else:
   print("Yes")
```
A. Yes
B. True
C. error
D. No

4. What will be the output when the following program is run?
```
tupl = 5,4,"Earth"
print(list(tupl))
```
A. 5,4,'Earth'
B. [5,4]
C. [5, 4, 'Earth']
D. {5,4,'Earth'}

5. What is the output of the following code:
```
def fun(*val):
   print(type(val))

lst=[1,2,3,4,5]
number = 400
fun(lst,number)
```
A. <class 'tuple'>
B. <class 'list'><class 'int'>
C. <class 'list'>
D. error

6. What will the output be after executing this code?
```
x = []
y = ""
z = -1

print(bool(x),bool(y),bool(z))
```
A. True True False
B. False False True

C. False True False

D. False False False

7. What is the output of the following print statement ?

p = 10

q = 10

print(p is q)

A. False

B. True

C. SyntaxError

D. 10

8. What is the output when the following code is executed:

vowels = ["a", "e", "i", "o", "u"]

all = list(range(-2)) + vowels

print(all)

A. ['o', 'u']

B. ['a', 'e', 'i']

C. ['a', 'e', 'i', 'o', 'u', 'a', 'e', 'i', 'o', 'u']

D. ['a', 'e', 'i', 'o', 'u']

9. What will be the output after running the following code?

val = ['Python', 'Tuple']

val_t = tuple(val)

val_t.pop()

print(val_t)

A. AttributeError

B. ['Tuple']

C. []

D. ['Python']

10. What do we need to change in order to fix the following code:

str = "Peter "Piper" Picked A Peck Of Picked "Pepper""

print(str)

A. error as the variable name str is invalid

B. None of the above

C. Wrap the whole sentence in a single quotes and leave Piper and Pepper in double quotes as is

D. Escape the quotes around Piper and Pepper words using the \ character.

The two ways to fix the code are:
str = "Peter \"Piper\" Picked A Peck Of Picked \"Pepper\""
str = 'Peter "Piper" Picked A Peck Of Picked "Pepper"'

11. What would the following program print to the console when user inputs 3 and 'Python' to be stored in the a and b variables respectively?
a = int(input())
b = input()
print(a*b)
A. "Python Python Python"
B. Python
C. PythonPythonPython
D. SyntaxError


12. What do you expect the following code to produce?
greeting = "Good Morning"
for ch in greeting:
  if ch == 'o':
   break
  print(ch)
else:
  print("Good Night")
A. G
B. Good Night
C. Good Morning
D. Go

13. What will be the output after running the following code?
tuple_one = (1, 2, 3)
tuple_two = ("Apples", "Bananas")
tuple_three = (tuple_one + tuple_two)
print(tuple_three)
A. (1, 2, 3, 'Apples', 'Bananas')
B. SyntaxError
C. (1, 2, 3)('Apples', 'Bananas')
D. ('Apples', 'Bananas', 1, 2, 3)

14. Given x and y are two binary numbers, what would the AND (&) operator on these number yield?

Note, the bin() function will take a decimal number as an argument and produce a binary number.
x = 0b101
y = 0b110
print(bin(x & y))
A. 0b110
B. 0b101
C. 0b001
D. 0b100

15. What do you expect the following print statement to produce ?
str = "Betty Bought A Bit Of Bitter Butter"
print('Butter' in str)
A. False
B. Butter
C. "Butter"
D. True

16. What will be the output after running the following code?
if not(True):
  print("hi")
else:
  print("bye")
A. False
B. error
C. hi
D. bye

17. What will the output be after executing this code?
h = {'blue': 1, 'red': 2, 'yellow': 3}
while len(h) > 2:
  print(h)
A. error
B. The program will infinitely print {'blue' : 1,'red' : 2,'yellow': 3} .
C. {'blue' : 1,'red' : 2,'yellow': 3}
D. Nothing is printed

18. What do you expect the following code to print out:
print(5 % 4 ** 2 // 2)
A. 1
B. 2

C. 5

D. error

19. What will be the output when the following program is run?

```python
print("Hello","World", end=" ")
print("Python")
```

A. Hello World Python

B. Hello World

C. HelloWorld Python

D. HelloWorldPython

20. What will be the output after running the following code?

```python
a = 1
b = 1
while a < 2:
  while b < 2:
    print(a, ":", b)
    b += 1
    a += 1
```

A. 1 : 1

B. 1 : 2

C. 2 : 2

D. 2 : 1

21. What will be the output after running the following code?

```python
def func(x,y):
    return x+y
print(func(9))
```

A. 9

B. 9+y

C. 0

D. error

22. What will the output be after executing the following code?

```python
fruits = ["apples","bananas"]
for i in range(1,2):
  for fruit in fruits:
    print(i, fruit)
```

A.

apples

bananas

B. error

C.
1 apples
1 bananas

D.
1 apples
2 bananas

23. What is the output of the following print statement:
greeting = "Knowledge Is Power"
print(greeting[::])
A.  Knowledge Is Power
B.  KnowledgeIsPower
C.  error
D.  "Knowledge Is Power"

24. What will be the output after running the following code?
languages = {'lang1': {1: 'Python'},
      'lang2': {2: 'Java'}}
print (languages['lang1'][1])
A.  error
B.  Java
C.  Python
D.  1

25. What will the output be when the following code is executed?
def func(val1 = 2, val2 = 4):
   print(val1 + val2)
func(val2 = 3)
A.  Invalid input
B.  5
C.  6
D.  7

26. What will be the output after running the following code?
numbers = dict([('first', 3),('second', 1),('third', 2)])
print(numbers.pop('second'))

A. 1
B. [('first', 3),('third', 2)]
C. [('first', 3),(1),('third', 2)]
D. second

27. What will the output be after running the following code snippet?
```
a = 'Python'
i = 0
while i < len(a):
    i += 1
print(i)
```
A. 0,1,2,3,4,5
B. 6
C. 1,2,3,4,5,6
D. 5

28. What is the output of the following code:
```
def func(x):
    x = [1,2,3]
    return x

x = [4,5,6,7]
y = func(x)
print(x, y)
```
A. [1, 2, 3][1, 2, 3]
B. error
C. [4, 5, 6, 7] [1, 2, 3]
D. [1, 2, 3][4, 5, 6, 7]

29. What is the output of the following code:
```
def area_square(side):
    return side ** 2

print(area_square(10))
```
A. 40
B. 100
C. 20
D. 200

30. What is the output of the following code:

```
lst = [1, 2] * 5
print(len(lst))
```
A. 10
B. error
C. 9
D. 5

# Practice Exam 4

1. What will be the output after running the following code?

```
s = 0
for i in range(1, 10):
    s = s + i
print(s)
```

A. 45
B. 10
C. 1
D. 55

2. What will be the output after running the following code?

```
def func(mylist):
    mylist[3]="strawberries"

lst = ["bananas","apples","pears","peas"]
func(lst)
print(lst)
```

A. ['bananas', 'apples', 'strawberries', 'peas']
B. ['bananas', 'apples', 'pears', 'strawberries']
C. ['bananas', 'apples', 'strawberries']
D. ['strawberries', 'strawberries', 'strawberries']

3. What will be the output after running the following code?

```
def func(x, y = 6):
    return x ** 3
print(func( 2 ))
```

A. 8
B. 27
C. 216
D. error

4. What will be the output after running the following code?

```
for i in range(1):
    for j in range(1):
        print(i,j)
```

A. 1 1
B. error

C. 0 0
D. 0 1

5. What does the following code do:
```
print( 1 ** 4 // 2)
```
A. 2.0
B. 0.5
C. 0
D. 2

6. What will be the output after running the following code?
```
x = 2
y = 1.0
print(x+y)
```
A. 3.0
B. 3
C. TypeError
D. 21.0

7. What will be the output after running the following code?
```
val = 8
while val > 0:
    val = val - 2
    if val <= 5:
        print(val, end="")
        break
print('hi')
```
A. 8hi
B. 2hi
C. hi
D. 4hi

8. Mark the correct sentences about the break statement in a for loop (check all that apply):
A. Break statement alters the flow of the loop
B. Break will terminate the current iteration but will resume with the next iteration
C. Break will terminate the entire loop
D. Break statement in an inner loop will terminate the both inner and outer loop

9. What will be the output after running the following code?
```
a = 'python'
i = 0
while i < len(a):
 i += 1
 pass
print('Value of i :', i)
```
A.  Value of i : i
B.  Value of i : 6
C.  6
D.  SyntaxError

10. What will be the output after running the following code?
```
p = 0b1100
q = 0b1101
print(bin(p | q))
```
A.  0b1110
B.  0b1111
C.  0b1101
D.  0b1100

11. What will be the output after running the following code?
```
a = ["Monday", "Wednesday", "Thursday"]
a.insert(1,"Tuesday")
a.append("Friday")
print(a)
```
A.  ["Tuesday", "Monday", "Wednesday", "Thursday", "Friday"]
B.  [ "Monday", "Tuesday, "Wednesday", "Thursday", "Friday"]
C.  ["Monday", "Wednesday", "Thursday"]
D.  ["Tuesday","Friday", "Monday", "Wednesday", "Thursday"]

12. What is the output of the code below:
```
x = 30
def change_me():
 global x
 x += 30
 print(30 + x)
change_me()
print(x)
```

A.
60
90

B.
90
60

C. 90
D. 60

13. What will be the output after running the following code?
```python
def fun(data, *num ):
    print(data)

fun("Earth", 2, True, "Jupiter")
```
A.  Earth
B.  Earth Jupiter
C.  2
D.  2 True

14. What will be the output after the following code is executed?
```python
print("Hello","World",sep=None)
```
A.  Hello World
B.  HelloWorld
C.  HelloNoneWorld
D.  Hello,World

15. What will be the output after running the following code?
```python
tupl1 = (-1, 0, 1)
tupl2 = ('bananas')
tupl3 = (tupl1, tupl2)
print(tupl3)
```
A.  ((-1, 0, 1), 'bananas')
B.  (-1, 0, 1, 'bananas')
C.  (-1, 0, 1)('bananas')
D.  ('bananas', (-1, 0, 1))

16. What will be the output after running the following code?
```python
def fun(x=5,y):
    return x/y
```

```
print(fun(2))
```
A. 2
B. 0.4
C. SyntaxError
D. 2.5

17. What will be the output after running the following code?
```
temp = "True"
while not temp:
    print("Temp")
else:
    print("Fixed")
```
A. Fixed
B. Temp
C. error
D. True

18. What is the output of this code when 'Robert' and 13 are entered by the user and stored in variables name and age, respectively?
```
name = input()
age = int(input())

print(name, type(age))
```
A. Robert <class 'int'>
B. Robert 13(int)
C. Robert 13
D. SyntaxError

19. What will be the output after running the following code?
```
for i in range(3):
    print(i, end=" ")
print(i)
```
A. 0 1 2
B. 1 2 3
C. 0 1 2 2
D. 0 1 2 3

20. What will be the output after the following code is executed?
```
def func(num):
    if num %2 == 0:
        return True
```

```
    else:
        return False
```

```
x = func(2)
print(not x)
```
A. not True
B. False
C. not False
D. True

21. What will be the output after running the following code?
```
d = {}
d[0] = 'Python'
d['weekends'] = ["Saturday","Sunday"]
print(d)
```
A. ['Python', 'weekends', ['Saturday', Sunday']]
B. {'Python', ["Saturday", "Sunday"]}
C. IndexError
D. {0: 'Python', 'weekends': ['Saturday', 'Sunday']}

22. What will be the output of the following code?
```
print()
```
A. A blank space
B. error
C. A blank line
D. Nothing is printed

23. What is the output when the following program is executed?
```
data = [1, 2, "apples", 3.14, True]
del data[:2]
print(data)
```
A. [3.14, True]
B. ['apples', 3.14, True]
C. [1, "apples", 3.14, True]
D. [1, 2, "apples"]

24. What do you expect the following code to produce:
```
name = ""
while name:
 print("Good Morning")
else:
```

```
print("Good Night")
```
A. error
B. Good Morning
C. Good Night
D. Good name=""

25. What will be the output after running the following code?
```
def fun(a,b,c):
    return a * b * c
print(fun(c=2,a=3,b=6))
```
A. 36
B. 30
C. error
D. invalid input

26. Is this the correct way to write the code?
```
x = 1

if (x < 3): print("True")
else: print("False")
```
A. No, the syntax is incorrect.
B. Yes, the syntax is correct.

27. What will be the output after running the following code?
```
s1 = "Hello"
s2 = "hello"
print(s1.lower() == s2.lower())
```
A. False
B. True
C. error
D. hello

28. What will be the output after running the following code?
```
a = [1, 2, 3]
a.append(2)
a.append(1)
print(a)
```
A. [1, 2, 3, 2, 1]
B. [1, 1, 2, 2, 3]
C. [1, 2, 3, 1, 2]
D. error

29. What will be the output after running the following code?
dict1 = {"John":1234, "Fruit":"Apples"}
dict2 = {"Fruit":"Apples", "John":1234}
print(dict1 == dict2)
A. not equal
B. False
C. True
D. equal

30. What will be the output after running the following code?
tupl = ('Python','World') * 2
print(tupl)
A. ('Python', 'World', 'Python', 'World')
B. error
C. ('Python', 'World')('Python', 'World',)
D. ('Python', 'World', 2)

# Practice Exam 5

1. Which of the following statements is incorrect:
A. An indentation in Python language is mandatory
B. The '#' is used as single line comments and the """ """ (triple quote) is used as multi-line comments
C. We don't need to declare the type of a variable in Python program
D. All the above

2. What will the output be when the following code is executed?
name, phone, location = "Robert", 123455667, "Dar es salaam"
print(name, phone, location)
A.  "Robert, 123455667, Dar es salaam "
B.  Robert 123455667 Dar es salaam
C.  SyntaxError
D.  Robert' 123455667 'Dar es salaam '

3. What will be the output when the following code is executed?
print(end="\n\n\n",sep=":")
A. \n:\n:\n

B.
   :
   :
   :

C. Three blank lines
D. error

4. What will be the output when the following code is executed?
area = 25.6
area = int(area)
print(area)
A.  25
B.  256
C.  error
D.  25.6

5. Which of the following statements is incorrect (select all that apply):
A. The bool("123") will return True
B. The bool("") will return True
C. The bool({}) will return False
D. The bool(-1) will return False

6. What would be the output of the following code: print(2 % 5 ** 2)
A.  1
B.  2
C.  4
D.  25

7. What will be the output when the following code is executed?
p = 10
q = 20
r = 30

if p > 10 and q > 20 and r > 30:
    print("True")
else:
    print("False")
A.  False
B.  True
C.  SyntaxError
D.  error

8. What will be the output when the follownig code is executed?
val1 = 0b111
val2 = val1 << 2

print(bin(val2))
A.  0b00111
B.  0b11111
C.  0b11110
D.  0b11100

9. What will be the output of the following print statements?
lst1 = [2,4,6]
lst2 = [2,4,6]

print(lst1 is lst2)

print(lst1 == lst2)

A.
False
True

B.
True
True

C.
False
False

D.
True
False

10. What will be the output when the follownig code is executed?
```
val1 = int(input())
print(len(val1))
```
A.  error
B.  Type Error: object of type 'int' has no len()
C.  4
D.  0

11. What will be the output of the following print statement?
```
str = "Hello Python!"
str = str[-7:len(str)]
print(str)
```
A.  Hello P
B.  str is a keyword so the assignment isn't valid
C.  Python!
D.  Hello Python!

12. What is the output of the following code snippet:
```
fruits = ("Apples", "Oranges", "Bananas")
a, b, c = fruits
print(b)
```
A.  Oranges
B.  'Apple', 'Oranges', 'Bananas'

C. Bananas

D. error

13. What will be the output of the following print statement?
```
tupl1 = (1., 2., 3.)
tupl2 = ("Earth", "Mars", "Jupiter")
x = (tupl1 + tupl2)[-3]
print(x)
```
A. 3

B. error

C. 1.,2.,3.

D. 'Earth'

14. Which of the following statements is correct :
A. A tuple cannot be modified once created, as they are immutable by design
B. Adding tuples will produce a new tuple
C. The elements in a tuple can be accessed by using their index position
D. All of the above

15. What is the result of the following print statement?
```
groceries_list1 = ["Milk", "Cheese"]
groceries_list2 = ["Bread", "Butter"]
groceries_list1.extend(groceries_list2)
print(groceries_list1)
```
A. ['Milk', 'Cheese']

B. ['Bread', 'Butter']

C. ['Milk', 'Cheese', 'Bread', 'Butter']

D. SyntaxError

16. What is the result of the following print statement?
```
capitals1 = ["London","New York","Rome"]
capitals2 = capitals1
capitals2.remove("New York")
print(capitals1)
```
A. "New York"

B. ['London', 'Rome']

C. ["London","New York","Rome"]

D. SyntaxError

17. What would be the output of the following code when executed?

```
dict = {1:"iOS"}
dict[2] = 'Android'
print(dict)
```
A.  {1: 'iOS', 2: 'Android'}
B.  {1: 'iOS', 'Android'}
C.  {'iOS', 'Android'}
D.  {1: 'iOS'}

18. What will be the output of the following code when executed?
```
cities = {"UK":"London","France":"Paris","Germany":"Berlin"}

for city in cities.items():
    print(city)
```

A.
London
Paris
Berlin

B.
UK
France
Germany

C.
('London', 'UK')
('Paris', 'France')
('Berlin', 'Germany')

D.
('UK', 'London')
('France', 'Paris')
('Germany', 'Berlin')

19. What will be the output of the following code when executed?
```
a = 7
 if a % 2 != 0:
    elif a > 4:
      print("hi")
    else:
      print("bye")
```

A.  hi
B.  SyntaxError
C.  bye
D.  error

20. Is this the correct way to write the code?
```
val = 7
print("hi") if val < 15 else print("bye")
```
A.  Yes, the syntax is correct.
B.  No, the syntax is incorrect.

21. What will be the output of the following code when executed?
```
for i in range(1, 3):
    print(i)
else:
    print("hi")
```

A.
1
2
3

B.
1
2
3
hi

C.
1
2

D.
1
2
hi

22. What will be the output of the following code when executed?
```
for i in range(1, 4):
    print(i)
```

47

```
    break
else:
    print("hi")
```

A.
1
2
3
hi

B.
1
2
3

C. 1
D. error

23. What will be the output of the following code when executed?

```
i = 0
while i < 4:
    i += 1
    print(i)
    break
else:
    print("Break")
```

A. Break
B.
1
2
3
4
C. SyntaxError
D. 1

24. What will be the output of the following code when executed?

```
i = 0
while i < 4:
    i += 1
    print(i)
```

```
else:
    print("Break")
```

A.
1
2
3
Break

B.
1
2
3
4
Break

C. Break

D.
1
2
3
4

25. What is the result of the following code when executed?
```
def fun(x = 4, y = 5):
    y -= 1
    return x * y * 1
print(fun())
```
error
A. 20
B. 19
C. 16

26. What will be the output of the following code when executed?
```
def fun(x):
    x[-1] = "c"
val = ["a","b","c","d"]
fun(val);
print(val)
```

A. ['a', 'b', 'c', 'c']
B. ['a', 'b', 'c', 'd']
C. ['a', 'c', 'c', 'd']
D. SyntaxError

27. What will be the output of the following code when executed?

```
def fun(x):
    return ["Tea"]
coffees = ["Cappuccino","Latte","Macchiato"]
tea = fun(coffees);
print(tea)
```

A. Cappuccino', 'Latte', 'Macchiato'
B. ['Tea']
C. Cappuccino', 'Latte', 'Macchiato', 'tea'
D. error

28. What will be the output of the following code when executed?

```
def fact(num):
    if num == 1:
        return 1
    return fact(num-1)*num

print(fact(4))
```

A. 10
B. error
C. 24
D. 1

29. What will be the output of the following code when executed?

```
def grades(param1, param2, *grades):
    print(param2)

print(grades("Robert","Dar es salaam", ["A","A*","A+"]))
```

A. Dar es salaam
B. A', 'A*', 'A+'
C. Robert
D. Robert', 'Dar es salaam', ['A', 'A*', 'A+']

30. What is the output of the following code?

```
def fun(**names):
    for key, value in names.items():
```

```
    print(key, value, end=" ", sep=":")
```

```
fun(NAME="Robert",AGE=29, CITY="Dar es salaam")
```

A. Robert: 29: Dar es salaam
B. NAME='Robert, AGE=29, CITY='Dar es salaam'
C. NAME:Robert AGE:29 CITY:Dar es salaam
D. SyntaxError

# Practice Exam 6

1. What will be the output when the following code is executed?
```
print("London","Berlin","Rome","end=" " ")
```
A. London Berlin Rome end
B. London Berlin Rome
C. London Berlin Rome end=
D. London Berlin Rome " "

2. What is the output of the following code when executed?
```
def capitals(**val):
    for country, capital_city in val.items():
        print("{}->{}".format(country, capital_city))
capitals(UK="London",France="Paris")
```

A.
UK: 'London'
France: 'Paris'

B. {(UK -> London),(France -> Paris)}
C. SyntaxError

D.
UK->London
France->Paris

3. What will be the output when the following code is executed?
```
fruits = ("Apples", "Oranges", "Bananas")
fruit1, fruit2, fruit3 = fruits
print(fruit3)
```
A. ('Apples', 'Oranges')
B. Bananas
C. Oranges
D. error

4. What will be the output of the following code?
```
x = 5
def fun(x):
    x = x - (x-2)
```

```
    return x
print(fun(fun(fun(x-1))))
```
A. 4
B. 2
C. 3
D. error

5. What will be the output of the following print statement?
```
tupl = ("bananas", "apples", "cherries")
print(sorted(tupl))
```
A. SyntaxError
B. ['apples', 'bananas', 'cherries']
C. ['bananas', 'apples', 'cherries']
D. ['cherries', 'bananas', 'apples']

6. What will be the output when the following code is executed?
```
count = 0
for i in range(0,2):
   for j in range(0,2):
      count+=1

print(count)
```
A. 0
B. 2
C. 4
D. 1

7. What will be the output of the following code when executed?
```
def fun(a, b=1, c=4):
   print(a + b + c)

fun(1, 2)
fun(5, c = 2)
fun(c = 8, a = 3)
```

A.
7
10
12

B.

6
8
12

C.
6
10
12

D.
7
8
12

8. What will be the output when the following code is executed?
```
str1 = "Hello"
str2 = "HeLLo"
print(str1 == str2.capitalize())
```
A. True
B. False

9. What will be the result of the following print statement?
```
high_fives = [10, 0, 5, 15]
high_fives.sort(reverse=True)
print(high_fives)
```
A. SyntaxError
B. [15, 10, 5, 0]
C. [0, 5, 10, 15]
D. [15, 5, 0, 10]

10. What is the output of the following code when executed?
```
nums = [1,0]
for i in range(2):
  nums.insert(0,i)
print(nums)
```
A. [0, 1, 0]
B. [1, 0, 1, 0]
C. [1, 1, 0, 0]
D. error

11. What will the output be when the following code is executed?

```
name1 = name2 = name3 = "Robert"
print(name3)
```
A. name2
B. Robert
C. name1
D. SyntaxError

12. What is the output of the following code snippet?
```
a = 0
b = 1
while a < 1:
   while b < 2:
      print(a, b)
      a += 1;b += 1
```
A. 1 0
B. 0 1
C. 1 1
D. 1 2

13. What is the output of the following code when executed?
```
me = "apples",
print(type(me))
```
A. Invalid syntax since a comma shouldn't be there
B. <class 'tuple'>
C. <class 'str'>
D. error

14. What will be the output when this code is executed?
```
lst = [x for x in range(3)]
print(lst)
```
A. [1, 2, 3]
B. [3]
C. [0, 1, 2, 3]
D. [0, 1, 2]

15. How many times will  the character "*" get printed to the console?
```
x=1
if x>0:
   print("*")
   if x<2:
    print("*")
```

```
  elif x==1:
    print("*")
  else:
    print("*")
else:
    print("*")
```
A. one
B. two
C. error
D. zero

16. What is the output of this program after it is executed?
```
def squared(num):
  global sq
  sq = num ** 2

squared(5)
print(sq)
```
A. 25
B. error
C. 10
D. num ** 2

17. What do you expect the following code to output?
```
a = False
b = True

if a or b:
  print("True")
else:
  print("False")
```
A. True
B. False

18. What is the output of the following code snippet?
```
address_book = {'name': "Robert", 'age': 28, 'city': "Dar es salaam"}

while address_book:
  address_book.popitem()
print(address_book)
```
A. SyntaxError

B. {}
C. {"age': 28, 'city': "Dar es salaam"}
D. {'name': "Robert", 'age': 28}

19. What is the output of this code when 3.14 and 1.0 are entered by the user when prompted and stored variables in pi and radius, respectively?

```
pi = float(input())
radius = int(input())
area = pi * radius **2
print(area)
```

A. 3
B. 9.8
C. 3.14
D. ValueError: invalid literal for int() with base 10: '1.0'

20. What is the output of the following code snippet:

```
print("Hello","World")
print("Hello","World",sep=' ')
print("Hello","World",sep=None)
```

A.
HelloWorld
Hello World
HelloWorld

B.
Hello World
Hello World
Hello World

C.
Hello World
Hello' 'World
HelloWorld

D.
Hello World
Hello World
SyntaxError

21. What would be the output of the following code?
```
marks= [78,89,92,68]
def max_marks(marks):
    return max(marks)
print(max_marks(marks))
```
A. 92
B. 68
C. 327
D. error

22. Which one of these statements is incorrect:
A. 0o123 is an example of Octal number representation
B. 0X111 is an example of Hexadecimal number representation
C. bin(), hex(), oct() functions convert decimal numbers to binary, hexadecimal and octal numbers
D. bin() function will bin the values

23. What will the output be when the following code is executed?
```
b = 0b101010 << 2
print(bin(b))
```
A. 0b10101011
B. 0b10101000
C. 0b101010
D. 000b101010

24. What is the output of the following code when executed?
```
def add(new_value, values=[]):
    values.append(new_value)
    return values

vals = add("Toyota",["BMW","Mercedes"])
print(add("Ford", vals))
```
A. ['Toyota', ['BMW', 'Mercedes'], 'Ford']
B. ['Toyota', 'BMW', 'Mercedes', 'Ford']
C. ['BMW', 'Mercedes', 'Toyota', 'Ford']
D. SyntaxError

25. What will be the output of the following print statements?
```
ones = [1]
ones_again = ones.extend([11,111])
print(ones)
```

print(ones_again)

A. [1, 11, 111]
B. error

C.
[1, 11, 111]
None

D. [11, 111, 1]

26. What will be the output when the user enters 'quit'?
```
while True:
    name = input("What is your name?")
    if name == 'quit':
        print("Exit")
        break
    else:
        print("Hello, ", name)
```
A.  Hello, quit
B.  Hello, name
C.  error
D.  Exit

27. Which statement is correct regarding operators in Python?
A.  Bitwise AND operator returns 1 only if both bits are 1 else 0
B.  Bitwise OR operator returns 0 only if both bits are 0. If any of the bits is 1, it returns 1
C.  All the above
D.  Bitwise XOR operator returns 0 if both bits are either 0 or 1

28. What will be the output when the following code is executed?
```
greeting = "Hello"
def func():
    global greeting
    greeting = "Python"

func()
print(greeting)
```
A.  Hello Python
B.  Python

C. error

D. Hello

29. What is the output of the following code?

```
fruits = ["apples","cherries"]

for fruits[-1] in fruits:
    print(fruits[-1], end ="|")
```

A. apples|cherries

B. apples|apples|

C. apples|cherries|

D. IndexError

30. What will be the output when this code is executed?

```
ui_elements = dict([('radio_button', 2),('text_box',
3),('standard_button', 5)])
popped_element = ui_elements.popitem()
print(list(popped_element))
```

A. ['standard_button', 5]

B. [('radio_button', 2),('text_box', 3)]

C. ['radio_button', 2]

D. error

# Practice Exam 7

1. How would you insert a comment in python?
A.  #I am a comment
B.  //I am a comment
C.  // I am a comment in python //
D.  comment(I am a comment in python)

2. Who is the creator of Python?
A.  Anthony hopkins
B.  Guido van Rossum
C.  James Gosling
D.  Yukihiro Matsumoto

3. Which of the following is a wrong way to declare a variable in python?
A.  _ak = "forrest"
B.  123abc = "forrest"
C.  _myvar= "forrest"
D.  my_var= "forrest"

4. What kind of argument can you put into print() function?
A.  Only numbers
B.  Only strings
C.  All kind of arguments
D.  print() function doesn't support arguments

5. What is the output of below program?
```
print("hello world")
print("superman")
print()
print("wonderland")
```
A.
hello world
superman
wonderland
B. hello world superman wonderland
C.
hello world
superman

wonderland
D. none of the above

6. What will be the output of following code?
print("Lion king is a\ngreat movie")
A. Lion king is a great movie
B. Lion king is a\ngreat movie
C.
Lion king is a
great movie
D. Lion king is a great movie

7. What is the correct output for the code below?
print("red roses and violet roses")
print(" 'red' roses and 'violet' roses")
print("""red roses and violet roses""")

A.
red roses and violet roses
red roses and violet roses
red roses and violet roses

B.
red roses and violet roses
'red' roses and 'violet' roses
red roses and violet roses

C. red "roses" and "violet" roses


D. none of the above

8. What will be the output of mentioned below code ?
Dict = {'Name': 'Robert', 'age': 30, 3:[2,3,4,5,8]}
print(Dict)
A.  Syntax Error
B.  {'Name', 'age', 3}
C.  {'Robert', 30, [2,3,4,5,8]}
D.  {'Name': 'Robert', 'age': 30, 3: [2, 3, 4, 5, 8]}

9. What will be the output of mentioned below code ?
```
for num in range(1, 10, 3):
 print(num, end = ",")
```
A. 1,4,7,
B. syntax error
C. 1,2,4,5,6,7,8,9,10
D. 1,10,3

10. Which of the following the correct output to the mentioned below code?
```
print("apple","mangoes","Bananas","Oranges","Watermelon")
```
A. "apple","mangoes","Bananas","Oranges","Watermelon"
B. apple mangoes Bananas oranges
C. apple mangoes Bananas Oranges Watermelon
D. None of the above

11. Python is treated as a:
A. Compiled language
B. Assembled language
C. Interpreted language
D. None of the above

12. What will be the output of mentioned below code ?
```
print("bottle", "cup", "bag", "wallet", end=" ")
print("Mobile", "calculator","book")
```
A. bottle, cup, bag, wallet, Mobile, calculator, book
B. bottle cup bag wallet Mobile calculator book
C.
bottle cup bag wallet
Mobile calculator book
D.
bottle, cup, bag, wallet
mobile, calculator, book

13. What will be the output of mentioned below code ?
```
print("bottle", "cup", "bag", "wallet", sep="-")
```
A. bottle-cup-bag-wallet-sep
B. bottle, cup, bag, wallet
C. bottle cup bag wallet
D. bottle-cup-bag-wallet

14. What will be the output of mentioned below code ?
print(13//(2*2))
A. 3
B. 3.5
C. 4
D. Syntax Error

15. Which one is the correct file extension used for python files ?
A. .ty
B. .pyt
C. .py
D. .pt

16. What is the output of the mentioned below code?
if 2==2.0:
  print("same values")
else:
  print("different values")
A. different values
B. Same values
C. syntax error
D. runtime error

17. What would be the output of the below code?
fruits = ["Robert","Karamagi", ""]
fruits.remove("Robert")
print(fruits)
A. Robert
B. ['Robert', '']
C. ["Robert","Karamagi"]
D. ["Robert"]

18. What would be the output of the following code?
print((10*2)/5)
A. 6
B. 2
C. 1
D. 4.0

19. What will be the output of mention below code?

```
a= "castle"
b= "army"
c , d = a , b
print(c,d, sep="::")
```
A.  army::castle
B.  army:castle:
C.  castle::army
D.  none of the above

20. What is the output of the mentioned below code?
```
i = 1
while i < 10:
 i+=3
 print(i)
```

A.
4
7
10

B.
1
4
8

C.
2
6
10

D. Syntax Error

21. What would be the output of the following code?
```
temperature = 105

if temperature > 96 and temperature < 98:
 print("body is ok")
elif temperature > 99 and temperature < 103:
 print("fever detected")
elif temperature >103 and temperature < 106:
 print("Emergency, Rush to the hospital")
```

else:
 print("No data entered")
A. body is ok
B. fever is detected
C. Emergency, Rush to the hospital
D. No data is entered

22. What will be the output of mentioned below code ?
def myfun(num):
 if num >= 4:
   return num
 elif num<4:
   return 2

print(myfun(3))
A. 2
B. 3
C. Syntax Error
D. none of the above

23. What will be the output of mentioned below code ?

fruits = ("pineapple", "strawberry", "grapes", "orange", "kiwi", "cherry", "mango")
print(fruits[-4:-1])
A. ('orange', 'kiwi', 'cherry')
B. ('grapes', 'mango')
C. ()
D. ("pineapple", "strawberry", "grapes", "orange", "kiwi", "cherry", "mango")

24. What is the output of the following code?
aTuple = (200, 300, 400, 500, 600)
print(aTuple[-2])
print(aTuple[-4:-1])
A. 300
B.
500
(300, 400, 500)
C. None of the above
D. IndexError: tuple index out of range

25. What is the output of the following code ?
```
name = "robert"
print(name=="Robert")
```
A. TypeError
B. TRUE
C. FALSE
D. UnboundLocalError

26. What would be the output of mentioned below code ?
```
for num in range(1, 12, 2):
 print(num, end = ",")
```
A. 1.2.3.4.5.6.7.8.9.10.11.12
B. 1 3 5 7 9 11
C. 1,3,5,7,9,11,
D. None of the above

27. What will the output be after running the following code?
```
def magicTrick(num):
  if (num % 2 == 0):
    print('even')
  else:
    print("odd")

magicTrick(8)
```
A. even
B. odd
C. magicTrick
D. num

28. What will be the output of mentioned below code ?
```
continentOne = str("Antarctica")
continentTwo = "Antarctica"

print(continentOne == continentTwo)
```
A. FALSE
B. TRUE
C. error
D. undefined variable

29. Which of the following will convert the string "hello, life is beautiful" to "Hello, Life Is Beautiful"

A. capitalize()
B. uppercase()
C. bigcase()
D. upper()

30. Strings are immutable.
A. True
B. False
C. Maybe
D. So

# Practice Exam 8

1. Which one of the following is the legal way to declare multiple variables and assign their values in one line ?
A. a:b:c = "apple":"banana":"orange"
B. a,b,c = apple, banana, orange
C. a b c = apple banana orange
D. a b c = apple, banana, orange

2. What does tell() function does in python ? choose the best answer
A. it returns the current position of file handle
B. none of these
C. tell function is used to print the strings on console
D. it cannot be used in python

3. Will the below code run without an error ?
tupA = (2,6,8,9)
tupB = (4,6,7)
tupC = (6,5,2,1)
tupA = (tupA + tupB + tupC)

print(tupA)
A. Yes, the above code will run without throwing any error
B. The above code is illogical and it will throw an error
C. Some code will run, and some will throw an error
D. The error will occur if the user exits the program

4. What is the legal example of creating a function is python?
A.
def my_function():
 print("Hello there")

my_function()

B.
func my_function:
 print("Hello there")

my_function()

69

C. None of these

D.
function my_function():
 print("Hello there")

my_function()

5. What would be the output of mentioned below code ?
thistuple = ("Japan", "US", "Argentina", "Russia", "China", "Canada", "England")
print(thistuple[2:4])
A. ('US', 'Argentina')
B. ('Argentina', 'Russia')
C. ("Japan", "US", "Argentina", "Russia", "China", "Canada", "England")
D. None of these

6. What would be the output of mentioned below code ?
def func(a,b):
 return a + b + 3
print(func(5))
A. 8+b
B. 5
C. 0
D. TypeError

7. What would be the output of mentioned below code ?
tup = len((1, 2, 3))
print(tup)
A. 0
B. 3
C. 2
D. None of these

8. What is the correct way to create a variable a float value assigned to it?
A. float : x -> 1.9
B. x= float(1.9)
C. x= 1.9
D. x ->float : 1.9

9. What would be the output of the mentioned below code ?
_values = [1, 2, 3, 4, 5, 6, 7, 8]
print(_values[4])
A.  3
B.  5
C.  2
D.  4

10. What would be the output of mentioned below code ?
alphabets = ["a", "b", "c", "d", "e"]
word = list(range(0)) + alphabets
print(word)
A.  ['a', 'b', 'c', 'd', 'e']
B.  Syntax error
C.  0
D.  [0, 'b', 'c', 'd', 'e']

11. What will be the output of mentioned below code?
k = (4/2)*3

print(k)
A.  k(6)
B.  1.2
C.  none of these
D.  6.0

12. What python snippet will give 5 in result when you print it out?
A.  print(2+3)
B.  all of the given options
C.  print((2x2)+1)
D.  print((3-2)+4)

13. What would be the correct output of mentioned below code?
print("titanic", "was", "a", "huge", "ship", sep="*",end="|")
print("but", "sadly","it","sank")
A.  titanic|was|a|huge|ship|*but sadly it sank
B.  none of these
C.  titanic*was*a*huge*ship|but sadly it sank
D.  titanic was a huge ship but sadly it sank

14. What will be the output of the mentioned below code ?
val = 20

```
if val<40:
        print("less than 40")
else:
        print("greater than 40")
```
A. syntax error
B. less than 40
C. greater than 40
D. less than 40 greater than 40

15. How do you find out the data type of any variable in python?
A. x=type().('I am string")
B. x= (type("I am string"))
C. x= (typeof("I am string"))
D. x= (typeOf("I am string"))

16. What would be the output of mentioned below code ?
```
x = "Hello"
print(bool(x))
```
A. FALSE
B. Hello
C. TRUE
D. bool(x)

17. What will be the output of mentioned below code snippet?
```
myDict= {"House No. = ": "191", "country = ":"Tanzania"}
myDict["House No. = "] = ['street no.']
print(myDict)
```
A. None of these
B. {'House No. = ': ['street no.'], 'country = ': 'Tanzania'}
C. {'House No' , 'Tanzania'}
D. {'191' , 'Tanzania'}

18. What is the legal way to create an string in python?
A. my_string = str(89732)
B. my_string = "I am an string"
C. my_string =str("I am an string")
D. All of the given options

19. What would be the output of the mentioned below code?
e = {'books':2,'pens':2}
e['books'] = 3
print(e)
A. (3,2)
B. syntax error
C. {'books': 2, 'pens': 2}
D. {'books': 3, 'pens': 2}

20. which of the following is the right way to create a variable with numeric value 6 ?
A. my_var = "6"
B. my_var = 6
C. my_var = str(6)
D. my_var -> 6

21. What would be the output of the mentioned below code ?
def func(num1 = 3, num2 = 5):
   print(num1 * num2)

func(num1 = 4)
A. 4
B. 15
C. num1 * num2
D. 20

22. What would be the output of mentioned below code ?
x = 1
while x < 3:
  print(x)
   x += 1
A.
1
2
B. 2 and 2
C. 1 and 1
D.
1 and 1
2 and 2

23. What would be the output of mentioned below code ?

```
def volume_cube(side):
 return side ** 3

print(volume_cube(4))
```
A.  4
B.  16
C.  12
D.  64

24. What would be the output of mentioned below code ?
```
prog_lang = ['Python', 'JavaScript', 'C++', 'Ruby', 'C']
prog_lang.pop(0)
print(prog_lang)
```
A.  0
B.  ['Javascript', 'C++']
C.  ['Python', 'Javascript', 'C++', 'Ruby', 'C']
D.  ['Javascript', 'C++', 'Ruby', 'C']

25. What would be the output of the mentioned below code ?
```
tuple_one1 = (1, 2, 3, 4)
tuple_two2 = ("Japan", "Korea")
tuple_three3 = (tuple_one1 + tuple_two2)
print(tuple_three3)
```
A.  None of these
B.  syntax error
C.  (1, 2, 3, 4, 'Japan', 'Korea')
D.  (1 2 3 4 Japan Korea)

26. What would be the correct output of mentioned below code?
```
def fun(x, y):
    return y ** x
print(fun(2,3))
```
A.  0
B.  16
C.  8
D.  9

27. What will be the output of mentioned below code?
```
k = 12
d = 14
e = k+d
```

print(e)
A. 8
B. 2
C. 26
D. k+d

28. What would be the output of the mentioned below code ?
x = range(3)

for n in x:
 print(n)
A.
0
1
2
3

B.
0
1
2

C. 0
D. 0 1 2 3

29. Which of the mentioned below statement is true about "keyword"?
A.  keyword are reserved for number data type
B.  keywords are used to optimise your program for better debugging
C.  keywords can never be used as variables
D.  keywords must be in a program for it to run

30. The operator // means _____ in python
A.  this operator doesn't belong to python
B.  it is used to initiate a comment in python
C.  it is used for debugging the existing code
D.  it is used as a floor division operator

# Practice Exam 9

1. What does the following code print to the console?
```
first_name, last_name = "robert", "karamagi"
print(f"{first_name} {last_name} is an author")
```
A. TypeError
B. "{first_name} {last_name} is an author"
C. robert karamagi is an author
D. A Blank Screen

2. What is the output of the mentioned below code ?
```
x = 3.5
print(type(x))
```
A. <class 'float'>
B. <class 'str'>
C. <class 'int'>
D. <class 'bool'>

3. What does the following code print to the console?
```
if 5 > 10:
    print("fan")
elif 8 != 9:
    print("glass")
else:
    print("cream")
```
A. glass
B. fan
C. cream
D. fanglasscream

4. What does the following code print?
```
def add(num1, num2):
    return num1 + num2

print(add(3, 4))
```
A. 3
B. 7
C. 0
D. 4

5. What does the following code print to the console.
```
letters = ["b", "a", "y", "a"]
index = letters.index("a")
print(index)
```
A. 2

B. 1

C. 0

D. 3

6. What does the following code print to the console?
```
if False:
    print("Nissan")
elif True:
    print("Ford")
elif True:
    print("BMW")
else:
    print("Audi")
```
A. Nissan

B. BMW

C. Ford

D. Audi

7. What does the following code print to the console?
```
if 1:
    print("1 is truthy!")
else:
    print("???")
```
A. 1 is truthy!

B. ???

C. None of these

D. Error

8. What does the following code print to the console.
```
evens = [2, 4, 6]
last_num = evens.pop()
print(last_num)
```
A. 4

B. 6

C. 2

D. 2 4 6

9. What does the following code print to the console?
```
languages = ["spanish"]
languages.extend(["chinese", "polish"])
print(languages)
```
A. ["spanish"]
B. ['spanish', 'chinese', 'polish']
C. ["chinese", "polish"]
D. ["chinese"]

10. What does the following code print to the console?
```
hair_color = "blue"
if 3 > 2:
    if hair_color == "black":
        print("You rock!")
    else:
        print("Boring")
```
A. Boring
B. You rock!
C. blue
D. black

11. What does the following code print to the console?
```
nums = [1, 2, 3, 4, 1, 4, 1]
print(nums.count(1))
```
A. 2
B. 1
C. 4
D. 3

12. What does the following code print to the console?
```
print(True and True)
```
A. True
B. False
C. True and True
D. True and False

13. What does the following code print to the console?
```
fruits = ["apple", "pear", "cherry"]
print(fruits[-1])
```

A. pear
B. cherry
C. ()
D. apple

14. What does the following code print?
letters = ["beach", "car"]
funified = list(map(lambda word: f"{word} is fun!", letters))
print(funified)
A. ['car is fun!']
B. ['beach is fun!']
C. ['beach is fun!', 'car is fun!']
D. ["beach", "car"]

15. What does the following code print to the console?
print("lion" == "cat" or 99 != 88)
A. False
B. True
C. lion
D. cat

16. What will be the output of mentioned below code ?
marks = str(6)
print(type(marks))
A. <class 'str'>
B. <class 'float'>
C. <class 'int'>
D. <class 'marks'>

17. What is the output of the mentioned below code?
print(bool("Australia"))
A. False
B. True
C. Australia
D. bool

18. Which of the following is true about Python dictionaries:
A. Dictionaries are mutable and
B. Items are accessed by their position in a Dictionary.
C. Dictionaries are used to call functions
D. Dictionaries can be nested to any depth

19. What does the following code print to the console?
print("mouse" != "mouse")
A. False
B. True
C. 0
D. mouse" != "mouse

20. What is the key difference between Python scripts and modules?
A. The main difference between a module and a script is that modules are meant to be imported, while scripts are made to be directly executed.
B. The main difference between a module and a script is that scripts are meant to be imported, while modules are made to be directly executed.
C. Scripts are short and Modules are long
D. Modules are simple and Scripts are complicated

21. What does the following code print to the console.
flowers = ["rose", "tulip"]
flowers.clear()
print(flowers)
A. []
B. ["rose"]
C. ["rose", "tulip"]
D. flowers

22. What does the following code print to the console.
bases = ["first", "second", "third", "fourth"]
bases.remove("fourth")
print(bases)
A. ['first', 'second', 'third']
B. ['first']
C. ['first', 'second']
D. ["second", "third", "fourth"]

23. What does the following code print?
def loud(sound):
    return f"{sound} is noisy"

print(loud("factory", "explosion"))

A.  TypeError
B.  {sound} is noisy
C.  None of these
D.  SyntaxError

24. What does the following print to the console.
```
result = 0
numbers = [2, 4, 6]
for num in numbers:
 result = result + num
print(result)
```
A.  2
B.  8
C.  12
D.  Result

25. Which of the following is the correct example of a dictionary in python ?
A.  thisdict = (brand->ford, model->Mustang, year->1964)
B.  thisdict = ("brand", "model", "year")
C.  thisdict = (brand:ford, model: Mustang, year: 1964)
D.
```
thisdict = {
 "brand": "Ford",
 "model": "Mustang",
 "year": 1964
}
```

26. What does the following code print to the console?
```
if "cat" == "dog":
   print("prrrr")
else:
   print("ruff")
```
A.  None of these
B.  syntax error
C.  prrrr
D.  ruff

27. What does the following print to the console.
```
word = ""
counter = 0
```

```
letters = ["c", "a", "r"]
while counter < len(letters):
  word = word + letters[counter]
  counter = counter + 1
print(word)
```
A.  "c", "a", "r"
B.  c, a, r
C.  car
D.  word

28. Which one of the following is the right sign to initiate a comment in python ?
A.  *
B.  {}
C.  ^
D.  #

29. What does the following code print to the console?
```
some_names = ["li", "fei"]
more_names = ["mike", "phil"]
print(some_names + more_names)
```
A.  ['li', 'fei', 'mike', 'phil']
B.  ["li", "fei"]
C.  ['li', 'fei']
D.  some_names + more_names

30. The Python interpreter takes the code that you write and converts it to the language that the computer's hardware understands.
Is this statement True or False?
A.  True
B.  False

# Practice Exam 10

1. What will be the output of mentioned below program:
```
x = range(3, 10, 2)
for n in x:
  print(n)
```

A.
5
7
9

B.
3
5
7
9

C.
3
9

D.
3
10
2

2. What does the following code return?
```
a = [x ** 2 for x in range(6)]
print(a)
```
A.  [0, 1, 4, 9, 16, 25]
B.  [0, 1]
C.  TypeError
D.  a

3. What does the following code print to the console?
```
print("I am Batman")
# print("give me food!")
```
A.  I am Batman

B. I am Batman give me food!
C. give me food!
D. SyntaxError

4. Which of these in not a core data type?
- Lists
- Dictionary
- Tuples
- Class

A. Class
B. Lists
C. Tuples
D. Dictionary

5. What does the following code print?
```
dress = ("sock", "shirt", "hat")
dress[0] = "pants"
print(dress)
```
A. pants
B. "pants", "belt", "hat"
C. TypeError
D. dress

6. What does the following code print to the console?
```
if 99:
    print("99 is truthy! Thanks for speaking the truth")
else:
    print("Well this is wrong")
```
A. 99 is truthy! Thanks for speaking the truth
B. Well this is wrong
C. 99 is truthy! Thanks for speaking the truth Well this is wrong
D. SyntaxError

7. What is CPython ?
A. A module of python to debug errors.
B. Its a programming language
C. The default implementation of the Python programming language.
D. C# Python

8. What will be the output of the following Python code?
```
print(0xA + 0xB + 0xC)
```

A. 0xA0xB0xC
B. 0x22
C. Error
D. 33

9. Which of the following will print the total numbers of 'A' in the word:
"HOW ARE YOU"?
word = "HOW ARE YOU"
A. print(word(A).count)
B. print(count(A))
C. print(word.count('A'))
D. print.A

10. What does the following code print?
```
from functools import reduce

nums = [
    [2, 2, 13, 15],
    [30, 45],
]

res = []

for i in nums:
    r = reduce(lambda x, y: x + y, i)
    res.append(r)

print(res)
```
A. [31, 74]
B. Both
C. [32, 75]
D. [2, 2, 13, 15]

11: What will be the output of the following Python code?
```
str="hello"
print(str[:2])
```
A. hello
B. olleh
C. lo
D. he

12. What does the following code print?
```
nums = [3, 5, 16, 27]
some_nums = list(filter(lambda num: num < 10, nums))
print(some_nums)
```
A. [3]
B. [3, 5]
C. [5]
D. [3, 5, 16, 27]

13. What is a correct syntax to return the first character in a string?
A. x = "Hello"[0]
B. x = sub("Hello", 0, 1)
C. x = "Hello".sub(0, 1)
D. x -> Hello(1)

14. What does the following code print to the console?
```
a = {1, 2, 3, 4, 5, 6}
b = {3, 4, 5}
print(a.difference(b))
```
A. {1, 2, 6}
B. {1, 2, 6, 7}
C. {1, 6}
D. {3, 4, 5}

15. What does the following code print?
```
letters = ("a", "b", "d")
print(letters[-1])
```
A. b
B. a
C. d
D. -1

16. What does the following code print?
```
def add(x, y):
    return x / y

print(add(6, 4))
```
A. 1
B. 2
C. 1.5
D. 10

17. What does the following code print?
```
stuff = ("mobile", "pen", "mobile")
print(stuff.count("mobile"))
```
A. 2
B. 0
C. 1
D. 6

18. In a Python program, a control structure:
A. Defines program-specific data structures
B. Manages the input and output of control characters.
C. Dictates what happens before the program starts and after it terminates
D. Directs the order of execution of the statements in the program.

19. Write down the value of x in output after executing the code given below:
```
def funA(a):
   return a
def funB(b):
  return b * 2
def funC(c):
  return c + 3
x = funA(funB(funC(1)))
print(x)
```
A. 4
B. 2
C. 8
D. 1

20. What will be the output of mentioned below code?
```
print('new' 'line')
```
A. new line
B. newline
C. Output equivalent to print 'new\nline'
D. Error

21. What will be the output of mentioned below code?
```
stuff = [
  ["aa", "bbb", "c", "d"],
```

```
    ["eeeee", "ff"],
]

biggest = ""

for i in stuff:
    for j in i:
        biggest = biggest if len(biggest) > len(j) else j

print(biggest)
```
A.  ff
B.  bbb
C.  eeeee
D.  biggest

22. Which of the following is an invalid statement?
A.  a b c = 10000000
B.  a_b_c=1000000
C.  abc=1000000
D.  a,b,c=10000, 2000, 3000

23. What does the following code print?
```
y = 55
def wow():
    return y

print(wow())
```
A.  55
B.  TypeError
C.  Y
D.  wow()

24. What does the following code print to the console?
```
a = {1, 2, 3, 4, 5, 6}
b = {2, 6}
print(a.intersection(b))
```

A.  {2, 6}
B.  {1, 2, 3, 4, 5, 6}
C.  a.intersection(b)
D.  SyntaxError

25. What does the following code print to the console?
print(6 + 6 / 3)
A. 10
B. 7
C. 8.0
D. 4

26. Which of the following will run without errors?
A. round(6352.898,2,5)
B. round()
C. round(45.8)
D. round(abc)

27. X = "1"
    Y = 10
Pick the code which will produce an error when executed if the values of X and Y are as given above.
A. print(str(X)+str(Y))
B. print(int(X)+int(Y))
C. print(X+Y)
D. print(str(X)+int(Y))

28. In Python, what is one function to output content to the console?
A. print
B. console.log
C. Echo
D. display

29. What code will give nsn in output? Select all that apply
a= "Tanzania"
b= "Australia"
c= "Canada"
A. print(a[0]+b[1]+c[3])
B. print(a[0]+b[1]+c[0])
C. print(a[2]+b[2]+c[2])
D. print(a[5]+b[2]+c[2])

30. What does the following code print to the console?

```
if True:
    print("wow awesome")
else:
    print("Oh Damn !!")
```

A. Oh Damn !!
B. wow awesome
C. "wow awesome"
D. "Oh Damn !!"

# Answer Key

# Practice Exam 1

**1. B.** The ** operator is used to raise the number on the left to the power of the exponent of the right. The expression is evaluated from the right to left, and therefore it results in 9**0, which is 9.

**2. D.** Tuples are immutable and cannot be amended once created.

**3. A.** The program will print '#' 3 times. The outer most if statement is false, so the if block is ignored, and the else block ( print ("#"*3) ) is executed.

**4. D.** The == operator compares two values. Python is case-sensitive. The value robert is not the same as Robert.

**5. D.** The loop will print Hello once before entering into else clause, after i has is incremented by 1.

**6. A.** The answer is ('Python', 'Tuple') because the tuple() coverts the list to type tuple, keeping the same list elements.

**7. D.** If the value of a variable is non-zero or non-empty, bool(non_empty_variable) will evaluate to True.

Hence the if clause is passed ( bool ("None") = True ) and 'Groceries trip pending' is printed to the console.

**8. A.** The list is passed to the function, which returns a list containing one element. The returned value is stored in y , overwriting the old value which was [0, 1, 2, 3, 4, 5]. The new list is then printed.

**9. D.** The program will print out {1: 'Python', 2: 'Dictionaries'} , which is the value of type dict that was assigned to the variable Dict.

**10. A.** The value stored inside word is Python , without a trailing space. The program will then print the same string 3 times, without adding a space in between the words.

**11. C.** The answer is [0, 1, 2, 3, 4, 6]. Even though the function does not return a value, it does change the value of the last element in the list x, which can be accessed and inspected outside the function.

**12. B.** The answer is {'Name': 'Python', 1: [1, 2, 3, 4], 2: 'hi'} . The print statement displays the key-value pairs in the dictionary. The values of keys in dictionaries can be lists, strings, or tuples .

**13. B.** For each of the element in lst1, every element in the lst2 will be printed. Hence 0 1 and 0 0 in the first iteration are printed in the first iteration of the outer loop; and 1 1 1 0 in are printed in the second iteration of the outer loop.

**14. C.** The \n is an escape character for a new line. The program will print Helloon one line, before shifting to a new line to print Python .

**15. C.** The title() method capitalizes the first letter of each of the words.

**16. A.** As soon as a return statement is executed, the function terminates and anything after that return statement will be ignored.

**17. D.** The expression inside the print statement will evaluate two statements, and will return True if both statements are true. Although the given age falls between 18 and 20, there is a not operator in front of the clause - which negates the value.
The first statement not age > 18 evaluates to False, and the second statement age < 20 evaluates to True.

**18. C.** The for loop will start from 1 and go up to (and not including) 10, with a step value of 2. Only the alternate numbers are printed due to the step value of 2.

**19. B.** In Python, strings are represented as arrays, where elements can be accessed using their index position.

The -1 is the first index from the other end of the array (i.e.: the last element), hence 3, being the last element in the string/array, is retrieved.

**20. C.** Dictionnaries are made of key-value pairs. The value at the second position is changed from Two to One.

**21. B.** The answer is [7, 6, 5, 4, 3, 2, 1] . The symbol [:] accesses all elements in the list. [::-1] accesses all elements in the list but in reverse order.

**22. C.** Since the a+b is not in parentheses, the * operator only applies to b and hence only the " fi " value gets repeated.

**23. A.** When outputting text to a console, the separator sep by default is an empty space. In this code snippet, the separator specified is a # . Hence, every word printed is separated by a #.

**24. D.** The floor division operator (//) gives out the quotient as a whole number and does not include the decimal part.

**25. C.** A single value with a comma is a tuple. The parentheses are not needed for representing a tuple.

**26. A.** Since the value 13 passed to the function is not divisible by 2, the else block is executed and odd is printed.

**27. B.** The answer is 5 10.  The function swaps the values of x and y within its scope but does not return anything. The values of x and y remain unchanged.

**28. D.** The answer is 5 1. The  function argument y is has a default value of 5, meaning that it is an optional argument when doing the function call. In the case where a value is passed as the 2nd argument, the passed value will be used by the function, not the default one. The function call default(1) executes the function with x=1 and y=5.

**29. A.** The tup1 + tup2 will combine to form a new tuple and reassign the new value to the variable tup1, which is legal. The final answer is (1, 3, 5, 2, 4)

**30. A.** The element Apples in the list will be excluded by the if clause, hence printing only Oranges and Mangoes , separated by the space delimiter.

# Practice Exam 2

**1. D.** The inputs were swapped duing the assignment. x is assigned the value stored inside b, and y is assigned the value stored inside a.

**2. B.** The if clause inside myfun will evaluate to true since the value passed to the function is >= 4. The if block will then be executed, and the value of 4 will be returned.

**3. A.** The element 'bananas' will be removed from the list, and will be replaced by empty element at its position.

**4. A.** The answer is [7, 6, 5, 4, 3, 2, 1] . The symbol [:] accesses all elements in the list. [::-1] accesses all elements in the list but in reverse order.

**5. C.** The XOR (^) evaluates to 1 if either of the bits are 1. If both bits are 0 or both bits are 1, it retuns 1. We represent binary numbers with prefix of 0b.

**6. D.** The answer is 90. The inner loop iterates 9 times and the outer loop iterates 10 times for every iteration of the outer loop. So the answer is 9*10=90

**7. C.** Elements at each position in each list are compared in order when using the ==. In this example, the elements differ.

**8. D.** Exponentiation has higher precedence over modulus operator, hence the above is evaluated 2 ** 4 =16, then 9 % 16 = 9.

**9. C.** The function does not return anything.

**10. A.** The value of the numbers are the same even they they are of different types (integer vs float).

**11. B.** The append() method inserts the given element at the end of the list, hence the value of 5 is added to the end of the list.

**12. B.** The variable x is a global variable, which means it can be accessed and manipulated from inside a function without re-defining it in the function scope. Hence, the x takes a new value after the glob function is executed, and is accessed and printed from outside the function scope.

**13. B.** The loop iterates over the length of the list (3) . The insert() method is used to add the values 1,2, and 3 at positions 0,1, and 2 respectively, moving up the existing list elements' positions .

**14. C.** The while condition evaluates to false as i is not greater than 3, hence the else block is executed, and No is printed.
In this specific example, the increments and decrements do not make any difference in the result.

**15. C.** The capitalize() function capitalizes the first letter of the first word.

**16. C.** The tuples will be added together to create a new tuple in the order specified.

**17. D.** The greeting function expects a name argument when called. However, this argument has a default value of "", so it makes it optional. Calling the greeting function without an argument will not fail, and the default value will be used inside the function.

**18. A.** The separator sep will add a comma between the positional arguments when printing them.

**19. D.** The given mark falls in the third class category, so Third Class will be printed.

**20. B.** Inside the tripler function, doubler function is called with 2 as an argument.
The doubler doubles the number and returs the result. The returned result is then reassigned to num which is then tripled and printed out.

**21. C.** The sep is redundant here as there is no input object to be printed.

**22. A.** The variable nums is a two-dimensional list. The for loop will iterate for a fixed number of times in the range(1). The loop is executed only once (when the value is 0).
Inside the loop, the new value of the initializer is set to 10, as it was multiplied by 10. The nums[i][j] is nothing but nums[0][0], which is set to 10, the new value of the initializer.

**23. C.** This way of expressing a conditional statement is known as "short-hand-if-else". This method is employed if both statements have only one line to be executed.

**24. C.** Dictionaries are made of key-value pairs. The value for the key 'one' gets updated to 1.

**25. C.** The separator is used when multiple arguments are passed to the print function. Here we only have one argument (same string is duplicated and treated as one argument).

**26. B.** The *val declaration means that the functions expects multiple arguments.
When calling myprint function, one can pass in any number of arguments. Arguments will be passed to the function as a tuple and printed.

**27. C.** The if clause evaluates to false, hence the else block is executed and Python is Awesome! is printed out.

**28. B.** The division using the / operator works as a floor division for integer arguments.

**29. A.** The elements in a tuple can be accessed using their positions (indices). Here, we are accessing the elements from the beginning of the tuple till -7th position. When we start counting from the end of the tuple, the -7th is the character 'n', hence we retrieve characters from 'P' till 'n'.

**30. B.** The function expects two values. However, if not provided, the default values 2 and 3 will be used, for a and b, respectively.
Note that the function calculates and returns b to the power of a. When calling the function with one value, we are setting and using the

positional argument while the value b is defaulted to 2. The order of arguments

# Practice Exam 3

**1. A.** Here we are looking at nested functions. The function func1 will call the second function func2 , which in turn calls the third function func3.

**2. A.** The data from the list is accessed in reverse and includes every 5th element starting from the back of the list.
Other examples:
print(nums[::-2]) will print [7, 5, 3, 1]
print(nums[::-3]) will print [7, 4, 1]

**3. D.** The range function generate a series of numbers within a given range, in this case between 10 and 12, with a step of 2. In the first iteration, i is equal to 10, so 10 % 2 != 1  evaluates to True, hence the program prints No .

**4. C.** The list() function will convert the tuple 5,4,"Earth" into a list object.

**5. A.** The *val declaration means that the functions expects multiple arguments. When calling myprint function, one can pass in any number of arguments. Arguments will be passed to the function as a tuple and printed.

**6. B.** When bool() is provided an empty list, an empty string or the value 0 as an argument, it returns False. The expression will evaluate to True when bool () is given any other value, including negative numbers.

**7. B.** The is operator is an identity operator, it checks whether both the operands refer to the same object or not.
The p and q have equal values, stored in the same memory location, hence p and q are same.  You can use id() function to check if the variables are same: print(id(p)) print(id(q)) which will indicate the same ID for both variables.

**8. D.** The range(-2) does not generate any numbers. Hence, all is assigned the list of vowels, and printed.

**9. A.** This code will produce an error, since tuples are immutable and cannot be changed once created. The pop() method cannot be used on tuples.

**10. C, D.** Using double quotes in strings is tricky, as it is required as part of syntax to print the strings by surrounding them in double quotes. Fortunately, in Python we can use single quotes or double quotes. It is important to stay consistent.

**11. C.** When you multiply a string by an integer, a new string is returned. This new string is the original string, repeated X number of times by which it was multiplied.

**12. A.** In the first iteration, the program prints the first character, G. However in the second iteration, the loop is exited. This is because the program was instructed to break out of the loop as soon as it encounters the character 'o'. Hence, nothing is printed after the first iteration.

**13. A.** Adding two tuples together will produce a new tuple, which is a combination of the original tuples.

**14. D.** An AND operator evaluates to 1 if both bits are 1, otherwise it evaluates to 0. That is, 1 and 1 evaluate to 1, but 0 for all other three combinations: 1 AND 0, 0 AND 1 or 0 AND 0.

**15. D.** The in operator is a membership operator. It checks if the given value exists in a sequence such as strings, lists, or tuples. In this case, 'Butter' is found in str, printing True.

**16. D.** The correct answer is bye. Since the if condition evaluates to False, the first block will be ignored and the else block will be executed.

**17. B.** The length of h is 3, which is greater than 2. The expression len(h) > 2 will always evaluate to True, so the While loop will run infinitely.

**18. B.** The ** operator has higher precedence over %, hence 4 ** 2 will be evaluated first. The result of the first calculation is 16. The 5 % 16 // 2 will be evaluated from left to right, so 5 % 16 yields 5, and 5 // 2 results in the final answer 2.

**19. A.** By default python's print() function ends with a newline. By default, the value of this parameter is '\n', i.e. the new line character. However, we asked the program to end a print statement with a " " instead of a new line. This means that the next print statement will be printed on the same line, delimited by a space.

**20. A.** Both while loops will iterate only once. After incrementing a and b by 1 each, the conditions a < 2 and b < 2 will evaluate to False and the program will exit the loops.

**21. D.** The func() is missing 1 required positional argument, y. In the function call, only one argument was provided.

**22. C.** The outer for loop will iterate only once (it starts from 1 and goes up till but not including 2).
In this first iteration of the outer for loop, i will take the value of 1. The inner for loop iterates over the fruits list. At every iteration of the inner for loop, the value of i and the list element fruit are printed on the same line.

**23. A.** The start and end position indices default to beginning and the end of the string, respectively, and the step defaults to 1, hence the whole string is printed.

**24. C.** languages represents a dictionary of a dictionaries. The dict['lang1'] returns the value of the key lang1, which is a dictionary, and dict['lang1'][1] returns the first value in the retrieved sub-dictionary {1: 'Python'} , which is Python.

**25. B.** val1 takes the default value of 2, while the value of val2 is provided as an argument during the function call. 2 and 3 are added together in func, resulting in 5.

**26. A.** The pop() method was passed 'second' as an argument. Hence, it will fetch the value associated with the key second, which is 1.

**27. B.** The while loop will iterate as long as the variable i is less than 6, the length of the string 'Python'. For every iteration it is incrementing the i value, hence it prints 6.

**28. C.** The func() assigns the value [1, 2, 3] to x and returns it, which is is captured by y after the function call. The variable x outside the function scope is unmodified, and keeps the value [4,5,6,7] . Hence when printing x and y, we obtain the original value of x [4,5,6,7]  and the value of y [1, 2, 3] .

**29. B.** The area of a square is side raised to the power of 2. The function area_square takes side as an argument, and computes side**2. ** is the power operator in Python, hence 10 ** 2 = 100.

**30. A.** The list contains two elements, and when multiplied by 5, we are repeating the same elements 5 times. Therefore the length of the new list is 10.

# Practice Exam 4

**1. A.** The answer is 45 since the sum of numbers in the range range(1,10) amounts to 45.
(1 + 2 + 3 + ... + 9 = 45)

**2. B.** The list is passed to the function, which modifies the list by changing the element at position 3 to strawberries instead of peas.

**3. A.** The default argument (y) is not used in the function, the function returns the cube of the given non-default argument (x)

In this case func() returns 2 ^ 3 = 8

**4. C.** The outer for loop will iterate once, where i takes the value of 0. The same is true for the inner for loop, where j takes the value of 0. Hence the print statement print (i, j) produces 0 0 .

**5. C.** 1**4 gets evaluated first which yields 1. The expression  1 // 2 is then evaluated.

The floor division operator (//) gives out the quotient as a whole number and does not include the decimal part. Therefore 0 is the final result of the calculation.

**6. A.** When adding a float and an int, the data type of the resulting variable will a float.

**7. D.** The answer is "4hi" because the break statement forces the program to exit the loop as soon as val is less than or equal to 5. In this example, val is incremented by 2 at every iteration, going from 8 to 6 to 4, causing the loop to break. The value 4 will be printed, the program will exit the loop and prints "hi".

**8. A, C.** B is incorrect as the break statement inside the inner loop exits inner loop only and does not affect the outerloop, which will continue.

D describes the utility of the continue keyword

**9. B.** The answer is 6 because we use the pass statement to write empty loops. Pass is also used for empty control statements, functions and classes. Hence the pass statement executes all the statements and the answer is 6.

**10. C.** The | (OR) operator produces 0 when both bits are 0, else all 1s

**11. B.** The insert() method takes two values: an index and a value. It then inserts the value in the list at the specified position.

The append() method will add the element at the end of the list.

**12. B.** When we use the global keyword, the scope of the variable becomes accessible from every where in the program. The value of x is changed in the function by adding 30 to it. The new value of x is now 60. The print function does not modify x, it simply prints the result of the calculation 30 + 60 = 90.

However, outside the function, x takes the new modified value of 60.

**13. A.** The function is expecting at least one positional argument and the rest as multiple-arguments. In this case, "Earth" is passed in as the positional argument, so it is copied to the "data" variable while rest of the arguments provided are copied to num. The function only prints what is stored in data.

**14. A.** The sep=None behaves exactly as the default separator, which is the space.

**15. A.** The tupl3 was created using two tuples, however we did not use the concatenation operator. Instead, tupl1 and tupl2 were enclosed in a tuple (tupl1 , tupl2). This creates a nested tuple .

**16. C.** The non-default argument should be preceded by the default-argument, otherwise the function will throw an error.
```
def fun(x,y=5):
    return x/y
print(fun(2))
```

**17. A.** The while loop's condition of "not True" evaluates to  False , hence the first block is ignored and the else block gets executed.

**18. A.** The first text input Robert is s in sotred in the variable name , and 13 is stored in the variable age cast as an integer via the int() method. When printing, we print the name and the datatype of age, which is int.

**19. C.** The range() function generates numbers between 0 and 3 (i.e.: 0,1,2). In the for loop, the elements 0, 1 and 2 will be printed, separated by a space. When the loop is exited, the last element in the range is captured in i and printed.

**20. B.** The function returns True since 2 % 2 == 0. However, the print statement is expected to print the negation of the returned value (not True) which is False.

**21. D.** We are inserting data into our dictionaries by assigning values to the keys.

**22. C.** An empty print() statement will print a blank line. An invisible new line character (\n) will be introduced by default.

**23. B.** The del operator deletes the elements, in this case, from the beginning of the list until the element at position 1 (excluding 2).

**24. C.** The while loop's conditional statement evaluates to False: bool(name) returns False since bool of an empty string always evaluates to False), hence the else block is executed.

**25. A.** The answer is 36 because even though the arguments are jumbled, they follow the keyword values. Therefore, 2*3*6=36

**26. B.** When the if or else statement contains only one line of code, it can be written in the given format so the syntax is correct.

**27. B.** The lower() method returns a string where all characters are lower case. Therefore. "Hello" turns into "hello" and the two strings become equal.

**28. A.** The append() method adds the data at the end of the list, so 2 and 1 are added in succession.

**29. C.** The dictionaries store data in key-value format, hence the comparison between two dictionaries is on the basis of key value pairs having the same positions, and not solely on the values.

**30. A.** The tuple when multiplied by an integer produces a new tuple with the same elements, multiplied X number of times (in this example, twice).

# Practice Exam 5

**1. D.** Python is indentation-strict language.
We can use # for single line comments or triple quotes for multiple-line comments (usually called DocStrings).
Python is a dynamically typed language so we don't need to declare the variable data type.

**2. B.** Multiple variables can be assigned values as shown in the example above.
Keep in mind that we must have the same number of variables and values, otherwise we will get one of the following errors depending on the situation:
TypeError: cannot unpack non-iterable int object if the number of values on the right side is less than the number of variables on the left side.
ValueError: too many values to unpack if the number of values on the right side is larger than the number of variables on the left side.

**3. C.** The end = "\n\n\n" will append three newline characters (\n) after printing out the text. Since there are no objects provided to the print() function to be printed, only the three empty lines will be printed. The sep is redundant in this code as there is no text to be printed.

**4. A.** The int function will round down to the previous whole number, in this case 25.

**5. B, D.** The bool function when provided an empty string, empty object, or zero, will return False. In any other case, it will return True. bool("") evaluates to False as it is an empty string and the bool(-1) evaluates True as -1 is a non-zero value. For example, try running the following:
```
print(bool(123))     # True
print(bool(""))      # False
print(bool({}))      # False
print(bool(0))       # False
print(bool(-1))      # True
```

**6. B.** The exponentiation will take precedence over modulo, hence the above expression can be simplified to 2 % 25 . The remainder of the division of 25 by 2 is 2.

**7. A.** The if condition will evaluate to False as since p is not less than 10, q is not greater than 20 and r is not greater than 30.  Hence the else block will get executed.
Note: In this example, all of the conditions in the if statement evaluate to False. However in another scenario, even if only one of them is False, the if block would not get executed.

**8. D.** The left shift operator shifts the bits to the left by the given number. The current 111 will be moved by 2 bits with 0's filled in, hence 11100

**9. A.** The is operator is an identity operator, it checks whether both the operands refer to the same object or not. lst1 and lst2 are two different objects (despite their content being the same).
The == operator checks if the values stored in the variables are equal to each other, which is True in this case.

**10. B.** The len() function cannot be used on integers. It can only be used on sequences such as strings, lists, tuples.

**11. C.** The starting position is -7 and the end position is the len(string), which is 13. Hence the string extracted is from position -7 (7th position starting from the end of the list) to position 13.

**12. A.** The elements in a tuple can be unpacked and assigned to variables as shown here. In this example, we are declaring 3 variables, to which we are assigning the tuple. The first element will be assigned to a, the 2nd to b, and the 3rd to c. Hence the print statement prints out Oranges .
Note that the number of variables must be the same the number of elements in the tuple, otherwise the Python interpreter will throw a ValueError: not enough values to unpack

**13. D.** Adding two tuples will result in a new tuple with the values from both tuples combined.
We then extract the element value at position -3, the third position starting from the back of the list. This element is 'Earth'.

**14. D.** Tuples are immutable by design and hence the data cannot be changed once created. Adding multiple tuples together will produce a new tuple with all the elements combined. The elements can be accessed by its index.

**15. C.** The extend() method used on a list adds the second list to the main list, producing a super set of elements.

**16. B.** Both variables point to the same list values. Changing one variable changes the underlying list.

**17. A.** The dictionary was created with a key-value pair of 1: 'iOS'. We can add a new key-value pair in the following manner: dict['key'] = value

**18. D.** The items() method used on a dictionary fetches the set of key-value pairs. In this example, we will get all the sets as country-capital tuples printed out.

**19. B.** The right answer is SyntaxError. The syntax is invalid due to the elif block not having a matching if block before it (the identation of the if anf elif blocks is different).

**20. A.** When the if or else statement contains only one line of code, it can be written in the given format so the syntax is correct.

**21. D.** This program will print:
1
2
hi
In a for-else loop, the else block is always executed.

**22. C.** The answer is 1 . When inserted in the loop, the break statement terminates the loop and the program (in this case).

**23. D.** The answer is 1 . In this example, the break statement will terminate the loop after the first iteration.

**24. B.** The answer is 1 2 3 4 Break because the while loop executes until the condition evaluates to False, after which the else block is executed.

**25. D.** As we are not passing arguments to fun during the function call, the default values will be considered for x and y (4 and 5, respectively). Inside the definition, we are modifying the y value, by decrementing it by 1. Hence the calculation evaluates to 4*4*1 = 16.

**26. A.** Although the function does not return a value, it does change the list provided as an argument. The function changes the last element of index -1 by replacing it with the string "c".

**27. B.** The list is passed to the function as an argument, however it is not used in the body of the function. fun simply returns a new list cotnaining one element, which is captured by the variable tea and printed out to the console.

**28. C.** This is a recursive function, which calls itself.
First call: the returned value is 4 * fact (3)
Second call: the returned value is 3 * fact (2)
Third call: the returned value is 2 * fact (1)
Fourth call : the returned value is 1
The result is 4 * 3 * 2 * 1 = 24.

**29. A.** The *grades means that the functions expects multiple arguments. The positional parameters param1 and param2 will be assigned with the first two arguments, "Robert"and " Dar es salaam" respectively. The rest of the arguments will be considered as multiple arguments and assigned to the *grades variable.

**30. C.** In the function definition, **names is used to pass a keyworded, variable-length argument (name-value pairs). The names.items() will return both key and value of each pair.

# Practice Exam 6

**1. C.** The end=" " is not provided as a keyword argument, but just as another argument to the print function since it is enclosed in quotation marks, hence treated as a string.

**2. D.** The \*\*val parameter holds the name-value arguments as a dictionary. In the function, the key and the value are printed in the specified format.

**3. B.** The tuples can be unpacked into equivalent number of variables as shown in the example above. Each element in the tuple will be stored in one of the variables, in that order. Hence fruit1 stores Apples, fruit2 stores Oranges, and fruit3 stores Bananas.

**4. B.** In this example, we are calling fun() 3 times from inside the print statement. The inner function will be executed first, with a value of 4 as an argument.
The returned value (2) from this innermost function call is then used as an argument in the next function call. The result from the second function is finally fed to the last function call, which returns 2 .

**5. B.** The sorted() function sorts the given data structure alphabetically. The result is the original list, sorted in alphabetical order.

**6. C.** The outer loop iterates twice. For each each iteration of the outer loop, the inner loop iterates twice. Hence 2 * 2 = 4 is the count value.

**7. D.** Unless specified, the 2nd and 3rd arguments in fun() are set to take the default values so we only required to provide the value of a.
In the first case, the positional arguments a and b take the values of 1 and 2 respectively, and c defaults to 4, hence 1+2+4 = 7
In the second case, a = 5, b = 1, c = 2, hence the result is 8 .
In the third case, a = 3, b = 1, and c = 8, resulting in 13 .

**8. A.** The capitalize() function will re-write the word by capitalizing the first letter, and keeping the rest of letters in lower-case. Hence, the result is 'Hello'.

**9. B.** The sort() method on a list will sort the elements in ascending order.
However, should you pass reverse=True, the list will then be sorted in descending order. Hence, the resulting list goes from larger to smaller values: [15, 10, 5, 0]

**10. B.** The insert() function is adding the value stored in i at the 0th position for every iteration. Hence the 1,0 are added to the list at 0th index while the original values of 1,0 will be pushed to the right/end of the list.

**11. B.** We can create multiple variables with the same value using the above format (var1 = var2 = var3 = "Value")

**12. B.** The condition of the outer while loop will evaluate to True in the first iteration. Similarly, the inner while loop's condition will evaluate to True in the first iteration.
Hence printing out a's value from outer loop (0) and b's value from inner loop.
This short program will run only once, since after the first iteration, the condition a < 1 will not be true anymore due to the incrementation.

**13. B.** In the first line, a single element with a comma will be created as a tuple. Hence, the data type of me is a tuple.

**14. D.** This is a list comprehension, a way to define and create lists based on existing lists. We are creating a list by selecting elements from the range 0 up to 3, using a for loop. Each of the elements in this range is collated to make up the new list.

**15. B.** Every print statement is only executed when the corresponding conditional statement evaluates to True.
The first condition x > 0 evaluates to True, so one * is printed. The condition of the second nested if statement evaluates to True ( x<2) so another * is printed.
The elif and else blocks will be ignored since the previous if blocks were executed.
Hence only two ** get printed.

**16. A.** sq was defined as a global keyword inside the function, hence changes in the function are reflected outside the function scope as well.

**17. A.** The if condition is evaluated using the or operator, which results in True if at least one of the operands results is True. In this example, although a is False, b is True, therefore if block gets executed.

**18. B.** The popitem() method deletes the last element in the series. Hence all the items are deleted as the loop iterates through the elements in adress_book, resulting in an empty dictionary.

**19. D.** The variable radius is expecting an integer, however the user entered a float (1.0).
The int(input()) type casting fails.

**20. B.** All three print statements produce the same output. The sep= ' ' ,sep = None and no sep will all enable the default separator, which is the empty space.

**21. A.** The answer is 92 because max() returns the maximum value in a list.

**22. D.** The bin() converts decimal numbers into other number systems.

**23. B.** Left shift operator shifts the left operand by number of places given in the right operand by filling up with zeros.

**24. C.** The add() function appends a new value to the list given as an argument, and returns the new extended list. During the function call, the returned value is captured by vals variable. Then we are calling the add() function again from within the print statement, adding Ford, thus creating and outputting the final list ['BMW', 'Merc', 'Toyota', 'Ford'] .

**25. C.** The extend() method used on a list adds the elements of the specified list provided as an argument to the end of the current list. Hence ones stores [1, 11, 111] and is printed out by the first print statement.
However, the extend() function does not return anything, it operates on the list on which it was used (ones). Hence ones_again stores the value of None.

**26. D.** The if clause evaluates to True as the input matched with 'quit', hence Exit gets printed to the console.

27. C. All the above statements are correct.

28. B. The variable greeting declared outside of the function is modified inside the function by defining greeting as a global keyword inside func().
Any changes that were made in this function will now be apply in the global sope (i.e.: outside this function), hence "Python" is the output.

29. B. In the for loop, the first iteration fetches "apples", right? Usually we set this element on to a local variable - like for f in fruits where the f is the local variable. But in this case what we are doing is a bit weird - we are setting it to a variable called fruits[-1]. Now what is fruits[-1]. Isn't this accessing the element from the fruits list at -1th position? Exactly! That is, we are actually setting the first element fetched during the first iteration ("apples") to fruits[-1] which is nothing but the last element - this means we are replacing the "cherries" to "apples"!! We are actually MODIFYING the main list by running this for loop and assigning it to that local variable!

30. A. The dictionary is constructed by using tuples enclosed in a list. Popping an item from the dictionary will remove last element. Here we are capturing the last element in a variable by using popitem(), converting the element to a list and printing it out to the console.

# Practice Exam 7

**1. A.** # sign is used to initiate a single line comment in python.

**2. B.** Guido van Rossum is the author of python programming language. He started to work on python in 1989.

**3. B.** Variable names cannot be started with a digit.
Mentioned below are legal and illegal ways for writing a variable name:

Rules for declaring variable names:
1. A variable name must start with a letter or the underscore character
2. A variable name cannot start with a number
3. A variable name can only contain alpha-numeric characters and underscores (A-z, 0-9, and _ )
4. Variable names are case-sensitive (age, Age and AGE are three different variables)

Legal variable names examples:
myvar = "Robert"
my_var = "Robert"
_my_var = "Robert"
myVar = "Robert"
MYVAR = "Robert"
myvar2 = "Robert"

illegal variable names examples:
2myvar = "Robert"
my-var = "Robert"
my var = "Robert"

**4. C.** You can put all kind of arguments in print function. Regardless of their data type.

**5. C.** Each print() function utilises a new line in output. Even a blank print() function.

**6. C.** \n has been used to break the line of any string. You can use this inside any string to break the line in your output.

**7. B.** Because we are using inverted commas inside double inverted commas, python is not gonna ignore the single inverted commas. (see the second line)
Although, Triple inverted commas used adjacent to each others will be ignored by python and will be considered (as one as mentioned in third line.)

**8. D.** When we use dictionaries key-value pair will always be displayed when we print it out.

**9. A.** In this case the for loop will start from 1 and go up to 10 with skipping 2 digits in between because the step value is 3, if the step value was 2 then the result would be like 1,3,5,7,9,

**10. C.** print function which are invoked with two or more than two arguments output all arguments in one line after ignoring all commas and inverted commas, all arguments will be separated by a single space.

**11. C.** Python is called an interpreted language because it goes through an interpreter, which turns code you write into the language understood by your computer's processor.

**12. B.** by default the print function ends with starting a new line, so a new print function will always start with a new line but when we use end = "" in print function, the arguments of next print function will be in same line.

**13. D.** sep ="-" is used as a separator in between arguments of print command

**14. A.** The floor division // rounds the result down to the nearest whole number

**15. C.** .py is the standard extention use for python files

**16. B.** Because values are same, doesn't matter if they are even numbers or floats.

**17. B.** The element "Robert" will be removed from the list and will be replaced by the successor "Karamagi".

**18. D.** Because first we solve the bracket (10*2) which is 20 and then divide 20 by 5 to get the answer "4".
"/" sign means division sign in python.

**19. C.** Variable c took it's value from a, and d took its value from b. then after printing, both values are separated by "::"

**20. A.** A loop will be started with an increment of '3' each time till the series reaches the number 10, which is the defined end limit.

**21. C.** Because the assigned value to temperature is 105 which is is greater than 103 and less than 106.

**22. A.** Because the assigned argument to function is a number which is less than 4. The condition of our program says that if the number is below 4 then return 2. So "2" is the correct answer.

**23. A.** Negative indexing means starting from the end of the tuple. This example returns the items from index -4 (included) to index -1 (exclude) Remember that the last item has the index -1.

**24. B.** Negative indexing means starting from the end of the tuple. [-4:-1] means to select a range in between position -4 and -1.

**25. C.** Because the value of name variable was "robert" which is not as same as "Robert", Python is a case sensitive language.

**26. C.** We used for loops here which starts from 1 and with the gap of "2" it goes all the way up to 11 and all individual elements are separated by ","

**27. A.** Since we pass the value 8 into our function which is divisible by two, hence the number is an even number and if else statement printed out 'even' since it perfectly satisfied the above situation.

**28. B.** The answer is true because str is used to convert string/number data type into string so it has no impact on "antarctica" since antarctica is already an string. In other words words both variables are same

**29. A.** capitalize() will capitalize first letter of all words.

**30. A.** Strings are immutable. You cannot change the object itself, but you can change the reference to the object.

# Practice Exam 8

**1. B.** You can declare and new variables and their values just like that, separated by commas.

**2. A.** tell() is used to return the current position of file handle, tell() function returns an integer value and it doesn't take any parameter

**3. A.** tupA, tupB and tupC will combined together and they will become a new tuple which will be reassigned to tupleA, the process is legal and will not throw any error

**4. A.** You will use "def" to initiate a function in python

**5. B.** [2:4] means to return the values which are on position 3 and position 4.
Yes, the element on position 2 will not be printed, it will be skipped. Whereas element on position 4 will be printed, this is the behaviour python shows when we select a particular range.

**6. D.** Because the argument requires two values i.e values of a and b in order to return a value but we have provided only one value which is 5, so the program throws an error

**7. B.** len is used to calculate the length. total elements inside brackets will be equal to the length of tuple.

**8. B, C.** float() can be also be used to make python understand that something is float.

**9. B.** This will give the value of item on position 4, remember the counting is started from zero in lists.

**10. A.** Because list(range(0)) generates no outcome that's why when concatenated with alphabets, it has no effect on the outcome and we have the value of alphabets printed.

**11. D.** Simple mathematical operations, first 4 is divided by 2 then multiplied by 3 and finally the value of k is printed out

**12. B.** All operations will give the result 5. Hint: solve the expression inside brackets first.

**13. C.** All elements are separated by * and at the end | is printed to separate both print function

**14. B.** We used a simple if else statement here, since the input value is lesser than 20 so it satisfied the first condition and printed out "less than 40"

**15. B.** type() is used to know the data type of any variable, in this case it will give <class 'str'> in print output

**16. C.** The bool() function allows you to evaluate any value, and give you True or False in return, if your value has some sort of content then it will always be evaluated to TRUE

**17. B.** Because House No. has been replaced by street no.

**18. D.** When you use "str" property, anything inside () becomes string. So all mentioned methods are the legal ways to create strings in python

**19. D.** We used "dictionary" here, dictionaries involve key:value pairs, you can update the value of any key like we did, we updated the value of books to 3.

**20. B.** Both a and b will give the same results. int() is used to convert make sure that whatever number you put inside () is a number (float/whole number)

**21. D.** Because we have passed an argument in our function that will give num1 = 4, whereas num2 remain unchanged in passing argument. So when num1=4 passes into function it prints (4 x 5) which is 20.

**22. A.** This will print x as long as x is less than 3.

**23. D.** "side ** 3" means "side raise to the power of 3". so you passed number 4 in the function that's why it would give 4x4x4 = 64 as a result.

**24. D.** This will pop out the element at position zero, right now 'python' is at position zero so it will pop out python from the list.

**25. C.** Because tuple_one1 and tuple_two2 have been combined together. You can combine tuples like this.

**26. D.** ** means y to the power of x. which is (3^2 = 9). The function expects two arguments and we provide them as x= 2 and y= 3

**27. C.** 12+14 are added together to become 26. The result of 12+14 is assigned to the variable e, then we printed out the value of e (which is 26)

**28. B.** Because a loop has been started that has a range from 0 to 3, so the counting will start from 0 and goes up to 2, (as a rule 3 will not be included in the printed list)

**29. C.** Keywords are special reserved words in python which are used to define the syntax and structure of python language. We cannot use them as a name of any variables, functions or any other identifier

**30. D.** // is used as a floor division operator in python. the floor division rounds the result down to the nearest whole number.

# Practice Exam 9

**1. C.** "robert karamagi is an author" is printed to the console.
first_name, last_name = "robert", "karamagi" is an example of multiple assignment in Python. This syntactic sugar makes it easier to simultaneously assign multiple values. We could have also assigned the variables on separate lines.
first_name = "robert"
last_name = "karamagi"
String interpolation is used to embed the two variables in a string.

**2. A.** In python a float refers to a number that has decimal places.

**3. A.** "glass" is printed.
If the boolean condition associated with the if is False and the boolean condition associated with the elif is True, then the code associated with the elif will be executed.

**4. B.** 7 is printed.
The add function takes two number arguments and returns the sum of the two numbers.
num1 and num2 are referred to as parameters.
add(3, 4) is an example of function invocation. 3 and 4 are arguments that are passed to the function when it is invoked.
When the function is called (aka invoked), the parameters are referred to as "arguments". So num1 and num2 are parameters and 3 / 4 are arguments.

**5. B.** 1 is printed.
The index() method prints the index of the first occurrence of an item in a list. The string "a" is in positions 1 and 3. The index() method returns 1 in this example because that's the index of the first "a" in the list.

**6. C.** "Ford" is printed.
The first elif that is True will be executed when multiple elif statements are True.

**7. A.** "1 is truthy!" is printed.

1 does not equal True, but it's considered True in a boolean context. Values that are considered True in a boolean context are called "truthy" and values that are considered False in a boolean context are called "falsy".

**8. B.** 6 is printed.
The pop() method returns the last element in a list and removes the last element from a list.

**9. B.** ['spanish', 'chinese', 'polish'] is printed.
The extend method is useful for adding multiple items to a list. We could have used two append statements, but this syntax is more verbose.
languages = ["spanish"]
languages.append("chinese")
languages.append("polish")
print(languages)

**10. A.** "Boring" is printed.
This is an example of a nested if statement. The boolean condition for the exterior if statement (3 > 2) evaluates to True so we enter the inner if statement.
The boolean condition for the inner if statement (hair_color == "black") evaluates to False, so the code block associated with the inner else statement is executed.

**11. D.** 3 is printed.
The count method returns the number of times an element is in a list.

**12. A.** True is printed to the console.
The and operator returns True when both of the operands are True.

**13. B.** "cherry" is printed to the console.
Negative indexing is used to fetch items from a list, starting at the end of the list. "cherry" is in position -1, "pear" is in position -2, and apple is in position -3.
In this example, we can fetch "cherry" with either fruits[2] or fruits[-1].

**14. C.** ['beach is fun!', 'car is fun!'] is printed.
The map() function is used to iterate over every element in the letters array and append the " is fun!" string.

The map() function takes an anonymous function as the first argument and a list as the second argument.

**15. B.** True is printed.
"lion" == "cat" evaluates to False and 99 != 88 evaluates to True.
False or True evaluates to True for the final result.

**16. A.** str is used to convert the numbers and floats into string data type.

**17. B.** print(bool(" ")) is used to indicate if something exists inside the inverted commas or not. If you write anything inside the inverted the evaluation will be TRUE and if you leave this empty then the evaluation will be FALSE

**18. A, D.** Python dictionaries are similar to lists in that they are mutable and can be nested to any arbitrary depth (constrained only by available memory).
The other option is wrong because Dictionary elements are accessed by key. Unlike with list indexing, the order of the items in a dictionary plays no role in how the items are accessed.

**19. A.** False is printed because the string "mouse" is equivalent to the string "mouse".
The != operator returns False when the operands are the same and True when the operands are different.

**20. A.** A plain text file containing Python code that is intended to be directly executed by the user is usually called script, which is an informal term that means top-level program file.
On the other hand, a plain text file, which contains Python code that is designed to be imported and used from another Python file, is called module.

**21. A.** [] is printed.
The clear() method deletes all items in a list.

**22. A.** ['first', 'second', 'third'] is printed.
The remove() method deletes an item from a list.

**23. A.** This code raises a TypeError with the following message: loud() takes 1 positional argument but 2 were given. The loud function was

written to only accept one argument, but two arguments were supplied when the function was invoked in this example: loud("factory", "explosion")). The code will error out when extra arguments are supplied.

**24. C.** 12 is printed.
The for loop iterates over every element in the numbers list and sums them in the result variable.
for loops are similar to while loops, but they allow for less typing because counter variables aren't needed.

**25. D.** The correct answer reflects the legal way to make a dictionary in python. A dictionary is a collection which is unordered, changeable and indexed. In Python dictionaries are written with curly brackets, and they have keys and values.

**26. D.** "ruff" is printed.
The boolean condition ("cat" == "dog") evaluates to false, so the code block associated with the if is skipped and the code block associated with the else is executed.

**27. C.** "car" is printed.
The word variable is initially set to the empty string and a while loop is used to iterate over every item in the letters list. Each letter is appended to the word variable and the counter is incremented for each loop iteration.

**28. D.** # sign is used to write a one line comment in python.

**29. A.** ['li', 'fei', 'mike', 'phil'] is printed.
The + operator combines two arrays into a single array. The + operator performs array concatenation when both of the operands are arrays (["li", "fei"] and ["mike", "phil"] are the operands).
In previous lessons, we've seen how the + operator performs addition when the operands are numbers (e.g. 3 + 4) and performs string concatenation when the operands are strings (e.g. "big" + "law").

**30. A.** The interpreter is the program you'll need to run Python code and scripts. Technically, the interpreter is a layer of software that works between your program and your computer hardware to get your code running.

# Practice Exam 10

**1. B.** This will create a sequence of numbers from 3 to 9, but increment by 2.

**2. A.** [0, 1, 4, 9, 16, 25] is printed.
This code squares all the numbers in range(6).
This code is an example of a list comprehension. List comprehensions are elegant ways to create lists from other lists.

**3. A.** "I am Batman" is printed to the console, but "give me food!" is not printed. The pound sign (#) is used to make comments. Comments are added to code for human readers and aren't interpreted by Python.

**4. A.** Class is a user defined data type.

**5. D.** This code raises a TypeError with the following message: 'tuple' object does not support item assignment.
Tuples are immutable so items in a tuple cannot be replaced.

**6. A.** "99 is truthy! Thanks for speaking the truth" is printed.
99 does not equal True, but it's considered True in a boolean context. Values that are considered True in a boolean context are called "truthy" and values that are considered False in a boolean context are called "falsy".

**7. C.** CPython is the reference implementation of the Python programming language. Written in C and Python, CPython is the default and most widely used implementation of the language.
CPython can be defined as both an interpreter and a compiler as it compiles Python code into bytecode before interpreting it. It has a foreign function interface with several languages including C, in which one must explicitly write bindings in a language other than Python.

**8. D.** 0xA and 0xB and 0xC are hexadecimal integer literals representing the decimal values 10, 11 and 12 respectively. There sum is 33.

**9. C.** count() function in an inbuilt function in python programming language that returns the number of occurrences of a substring in the

given string. in the above question we are trying to figure out that how many times the letter 'A' is used in the string, so our count() function will help us in figuring this out !!

Below is the Python implementation of the count() method as an another example:

string = "geeks for geeks"
# counts the number of times substring "geeks" occurs in the given string and returns an integer
print(string.count("geeks"))
# 1 will be the output

**10. C.** [32, 75] is printed.
A for loop is used to iterate over each sub-list. reduce is used to sum all of the numbers in each sub-list and append the sum to the res list.

**11. D.** Explanation: We are printing only the 1st two bytes of string and hence the answer is "he".

**12. B.** [3, 5] is printed.
The filter() function is used to create an array that only includes the numbers less than 10.
filter() takes an anonymous function as the first argument and a list as the second argument.

**13. A.** "Hello" is the string whereas [0] will return the first element of that string. If we used [1] It would have returned the second character of the string.
Positions in string starts from 0.

**14. A.** {1, 2, 6} is printed.
The difference() method returns all the elements that are in set a, but are not in set b.
b.difference(a) would return set(). since all elements of b are present in a

**15. C.** "d" is printed.
Negative indexing can be used to fetch items from the end of the tuple. -1 is the last position in the tuple, -2 is the second to last position in the tuple, and so forth.

**16. C.** 1.5 is printed.

The add function takes two number arguments and returns the division of the two numbers.

x and y are referred to as parameters.

add(6, 4) is an example of function invocation. 6 and 4 are arguments that are passed to the function when it is invoked.

When the function is called (aka invoked), the parameters are referred to as "arguments". So x and y are parameters and 6 and 4 are arguments.

**17. A.** 2 is printed.
The count() method returns the number of times an item is present in a tuple.

**18. D.** Control structures determine which statements in the program will be executed and in what order, allowing for statements to be skipped over or executed repeatedly.

if, if/else, and if/elif/else statements are all examples of control structures that allow for statements to be skipped over or executed conditionally:

if <expr>:
    <statement(s)>
elif <expr>:
    <statement(s)>
elif <expr>:
    <statement(s)>

    ...

else:
    <statement(s)>

The order of execution of statements in a program is called control flow.

**19. C.** funA(funB(funC(1))) in this expression, funC will return 4 which will serve as the argument for funB which will then return 8 and this 8 will serve as the argument for funA. So

step 1:  x= funA(funB(funC(1)))  -----> funC returns 4, (c is 1 here as an argument so c+3 will become 4)

step 2 :x= funA(funB(4))        -----> funB returns 8 , (as b*2 =8 and b is 4 so it would return 8)

step 2   x= funA(2)                 -----> funA(2) return 8, (the passing argument is 8 which becomes the value of a)

So, x will finally get the value 8.

**20. A.** Explanation: String literal separated by whitespace are allowed. They are concatenated.

**21. C.** "eeeee" is printed.
The biggest variable is initially assigned to the empty string.
A nested loop is used to iterate the nested data structure and continuously update the biggest variable with the longest string.

**22. A.** Spaces are not allowed in variable names.

**23. A.** 55 is printed.
The variable y is defined in the global scope. Global variables are accessible anywhere in the program, including the local function scope.

**24. A.** {2, 6} is printed.
The intersection() method returns all the elements that are in both set a and set b. Both sets contain 2 and 6.

**25. C.** 8.0 is printed to the console.
Python follows the order of operations, so division takes place before addition. Six is divided by three and the resulting quotient is added to six.

**26. C.** 6352.898,2,5 is not a legal number so using round() function on it will produce an error, similarly you cannot use an empty round function, it will produce an error as well. We also do not round letters.

**27. C.** strings cannot be concatenated with numbers, neither they can add up to produce any addition. Either both of them must be integers to perform the addition operation or both of them have to be string for concatenation.
"strings cannot be added or concatenated with numbers"

**28. A.** print function is used in python to print the content in output.

**29. C, D.** a[2] will pick the third letter of the string assigned to a, since positioning starts from 0. so when we concatenate a[2], b[2] and c[2] together, it will join m+s+n together to form msn.

**30. B.** wow awesome is printed to the console. We can  use True and False directly as conditions